Northern Regional Library
1300 Foulk Road
Wilmington DE 19803

W9-BZU-026
of New Castle
County Libraries

Kickstart Your Career

'Jeff Grout has advised thousands of job candidates over a long and distinguished career in the recruiting business. If you're looking for some solid advice to push your career along, look no further.'

Richard Donkin, *Financial Times* columnist and author of *Blood, Sweat and Tears: The Evolution of Work*

'The title says it all. Make use of Jeff Grout's advice if you are fed up and keen to make more of your career, reputation and life. Straightforward and practical advice to use today.'

Mary Spillane, Image Consultant and Performance Coach

'An essential guide to tackling the job market today, *Kickstart Your Career* is an informative and thought provoking read. Jeff Grout's straightforward, clearly laid out advice is easily accessible and thoroughly comprehensive.'

Cheryl Bickerton, Channel Director, TV Jobshop

'*Kickstart Your Career* is a well written, informative and extremely useful book for anyone seeking a job. The authors ought to be congratulated on what is one of the best books in the field for people who are seeking their ideal career.'

Professor Cary L Cooper, CBE BUPA Professor of Organizational Psychology and Health

'. . . a unique and highly practical guide. Packed with insider tips, together with insights and advice from top celebrities . . .'

Robert Peasnell, UK Managing Director McCann-Erickson Recruitment Advertising

'Chock-full of straightforward, down-to-earth advice, with the added spice of some fascinating insights and tips from a range of celebrities and business leaders.'

Hamish Davidson, Partner & Head of the UK Executive Search & Selection Division, PricewaterhouseCoopers

'There are many books that purport to give job application and career direction advice, but *Kickstart Your Career* will undoubtedly become the market leader.'

Mike Dodd, Managing Director, Academy (HR Services) Group Ltd

'. . . whilst economies go through cycles that set the tone for the job market, this book is a timely reminder that it is individuals and the way they prepare, anticipate and behave that make a successful career.'

Terry Nolan, Senior HR Development Manager, Unilever

Kickstart Your Career

The Complete Insider's Guide to Landing Your Ideal Job

Jeff Grout & Sarah Perrin

JOHN WILEY & SONS, LTD

Copyright © 2002 by John Wiley & Sons, Ltd,
Baffins Lane, Chichester,
West Sussex PO19 1UD, England

National 01243 779777
International (+44) 1243 779777
e-mail (for orders and customer service enquiries):
cs-books@wiley.co.uk
Visit our Home Page on http://www.wiley.co.uk
or http://www.wiley.com

All Rights Reserved. No part of this publication may be reproduced, stored in a
retrieval system, or transmitted, in any form or by any means, electronic, mechanical,
photocopying, recording, scanning or otherwise, except under the terms of the
Copright, Designs and Patents Act 1988 or under the terms of a licence issued by the
Copyright Licensing Agency, 90 Tottenham Court Road, London, UK W1P 9HE,
without the permission in writing of the Publisher.

Other Wiley Editorial Offices

John Wiley & Sons, Inc., 605 Third Avenue,
New York, NY 10158-0012, USA

Wiley-VCH GmbH, Pappelallee 3,
D-69469 Weinheim, Germany

John Wiley & Sons Australia Ltd, 33 Park Road, Milton,
Queensland 4064, Australia

John Wiley & Sons (Asia) Pte Ltd, 2 Clementi Loop #2–01,
Jin Xing Distripark, Singapore 129809

John Wiley & Sons (Canada) Ltd, 22 Worcester Road,
Rexdale, Ontario M9W 1L1, Canada

British Library Cataloguing in Publication Data
A catalogue record for this book is available from the British Library

ISBN 0-470-84301-2

Typeset in New Caledonia by Florence Production Ltd, Stoodleigh, Devon.
Printed and bound in Great Britain by Biddles Ltd, Guildford and King's Lynn.

This book is printed on acid-free paper responsibly manufactured from
sustainable forestry, in which at least two trees are planted for each one
used for paper production.

Contents

Part III From Close Encounters to Closing the Deal

Acknowledgements

We are indebted to the advice of the following people who kindly shared their insights during the researching and writing of this book. We greatly appreciate their help. However, any errors or omissions are entirely down to the authors themselves.

Many thanks to:

Robert Peasnell, UK Managing Director, McCann Erickson Recruitment Advertising

Chris Long, Partner, Whitehead Mann GKR (Senior Executive Search Consultants)

Suzzane Wood, Partner and Head of Financial Management Practice, Odgers Ray & Berndtson (Executive Search Consultants)

Brendan Keelan, Partner, Howgate Sable (Executive Search and Selection Consultants)

Chris Tanner, Company Director and Independent Business Consultant (formerly Director of Training at Deloitte & Touche)

Alan Dickinson, Chief Executive, Jobsfinancial.com

Mary Spillane, Author and Image Consultant, Imageworks

Mike Walmsley, Managing Director, Pro-active Consulting

John Archer, Partner, Archer Mathieson (Search, Selection and Interim Management Consultancy)

Hamish Davidson, Partner and Head of the UK Executive Search and Selection Division, PricewaterhouseCoopers

Stewart Rogers, Managing Director, The Rogers Partnership Ltd

Des Gunewardena, CEO, Conran Group of Companies

Graham Perkins, HR Consultant and Freelance Career Counsellor (Formerly Manager, Executive Search and Selection Division, Deloitte & Touche)

Diana M Ellis, Head of Education Practice, Odgers Ray & Berndtson (Executive Search Consultants)

Tony May, Partner, Stork & May (Career Strategy Consultants)

Cary Cooper, BUPA Professor of Organisational Psychology and Health at UMIST

Hazel Bunston, Consultant, Penna Sanders & Sidney (Outplacement Consultants)

Jonathan R Ebsworth, Partner, Reid Minty, Solicitors

Mike Dodd, Managing Director, Academy HR Services Group

Gary Hoyte, Director, Gary Hoyte Consulting Ltd (HR Consultants) and formerly HR Director of Scope

Peter Jackling, Managing Director, IDA Independent Data Analysis

Terry Nolan, Corporate Management Development Manager, Unilever

About the Authors

Jeff Grout was, until recently, UK Managing Director of Robert Half International, the largest specialist recruitment consultancy in the world. During a professional recruitment career spanning more than 20 years he has found positions for hundreds of people.

Jeff's accumulated expertise in all aspects of recruitment and selection means that he is often in demand as a commentator, columnist and speaker on the subjects of recruitment, retention and motivation. He has appeared on television and has participated in numerous radio programmes. Jeff collaborated with the BBC in producing an interview training video and has run interview technique courses for a number of the UK's leading companies.

He is also co-author of two books, *The Adventure Capitalists* and *My Brilliant Career*, offering insights into the characteristics of career success and based on public interviews with high achievers from the fields of business, sport, media and the stage.

Sarah Perrin is a freelance journalist and writer, contributing regularly to numerous business and professional magazines. Her articles cover a broad variety of topics, including career development issues, personal and corporate profiles, business finance and management. She is also the author of *The Guardian Careers Guide to Accountancy*.

Sarah qualified as a chartered accountant with Arthur Andersen in London before travelling, temping and ultimately making a successful career shift into journalism, joining the leading trade weekly for finance professionals, *Accountancy Age*. She has been gainfully self-employed since 1996 and, in addition to her journalism, she also supplies her skills to commercial organizations needing external writing expertise.

Our careers should be one of the most rewarding elements of our lives. Waking up in the morning we should be leaping out of bed, filled with anticipation about the new challenges ahead that day. Why waste the majority of our waking lives in any other way? But entering the office, how many of us really feel a tremor of excitement at the thought of the day ahead? Not enough.

Who is this book for?

This book is for all those who want to kickstart their career, regardless of the reason and stage they have reached. We aim to give all of you the key tips for identifying where your best opportunities lie and how to build the career of your dreams, from one job move to the next. You might be a new graduate looking for your first serious, full-time job and wanting to start your career on the best footing. How can you be sure you are matching your skills to the opportunities available?

You might be a senior executive looking to move up to the next rung of corporate responsibility and personal development. You might be job-hunting because you feel you have learnt all you can from your current position, you want new challenges and you recognize that your career is an exciting adventure.

Maybe you are someone who feels you started your career on the wrong track, and want to change direction. You recognize that hiding under the duvet on Monday morning doesn't make the day go away. By starting from first principles, and thinking about your own skills and aspirations, we hope to inspire you to find a working environment that fulfils rather than drains your energy, to help you find a new role far closer to your ideal job.

If you are currently out of work, then we hope this book will give you new ideas and fresh motivation for the job search. We aim to give you an insider's insight to the key attributes that recruiters are looking for in job candidates – the skills, attitudes and approaches required to turn those rejection or 'no opportunities at the moment' letters into offered job contracts.

This book offers advice you can use throughout your career. In particular, we stress the value of networking for building strong career foundations.

> ### Kickstart Tip
>
> **Successful job-seekers are often natural networkers. In fact, people with extensive networks of friends, relations, former colleagues, old college mates, neighbours and so on are far less likely to find themselves short of a job opportunity.**

Jobs for life?

Developing the skills that help you get the job you want is more important than ever in today's world. The job for life no longer exists. Who receives a gold clock these days after 50 years' service with the same employer? Anyone at all?

Recruiting and human resource specialists often talk about the 'psychological contract' between the employer and the employee. In the past, this contract (a state of mind rather than anything written down) implied that the employer would look after the employees, give them long-term work and take an almost paternal interest in their welfare. In return, the employees offered loyalty and continued service over many years, even throughout their entire working lives.

That has all changed. In today's dynamic marketplace, where yesterday's successful company can be tomorrow's dinosaur, employers can no longer offer such career security to their staff. Similarly, employees no longer trust that their jobs will be preserved. Nor do they expect that their best interests will always be met by one company, but see opportunities to move from one employer to another as their needs and aspirations change.

This climate has developed a new type of relationship between organizations and those who work within them. The employer undertakes to offer work, including training and development opportunities, for as long as there is a market opportunity which that working role helps to satisfy. There is no expectation, however, that the employees will remain with the employer no matter what; simply that they will offer their best services while they remain part of that organization's workforce.

At the same time, the employee has to take responsibility for ensuring that their skills are up-to-date, making the most of any offered training courses and keeping an eye on the labour market. Making strategic job moves in search of new opportunities and challenges is an accepted part of that self-development.

This fluid environment, although potentially frightening to those uncomfortable with change, can also be an exciting one. It is possible to move from one job to a new and better one. You don't need to become bored with the same routine and the same faces round the coffee machine. The opportunities are there to build the kind of working life that you want.

Who dares wins: the rise of the career mercenary

The people who do best in today's employment market are the 'career mercenaries'. In our definition, career mercenaries are independent agents who make positive employment choices, moving from one organization to another, depending on the opportunities and the rewards available. They remain loyal to themselves, placing their employment needs as their top priority, although they provide their current employer with the best possible service they can, so that both employer and employee benefit from the new flexibility. The employer becomes, in a sense, the employee's client.

Kickstart Tip

Career mercenaries recognize that they must take responsibility for their own career development, moving from one workplace to the next when the time is right for them, although if a single employer manages to fulfil all their career needs, all well and good.

You can be a good career mercenary and remain with one organization throughout your working life should you so wish. However, the career mercenary still makes an effort to develop the skills that will be in demand and watches the job market to spot where new opportunities may lie in future.

In writing this book we aim to explain how to become a successful career mercenary. You don't have to be ruthless or aggressive, but you do have to be clear-sighted about what you want and assertive in setting out to achieve it.

For most people, developing a successful career isn't something that just happens. Those who achieve what they want from their working lives usually do so by making a series of appropriate choices, through luck or wisdom, along the way. Building a career therefore relies on assessing what you want, what you have to offer and understanding what employers seek from you. It takes thorough research and careful planning to move from one desired state to the next. It may also require patience. Say you want to move from a line management role in one company to a marketing role in another; you will probably have to do so in two stages – changing role first and then company, or vice versa – rather than making both changes at once.

Risk and opportunity

One word of warning for the job-seeker. Change inevitably involves some risk. There's the old saying about better the devil you know. Your employer may have faults, but you will probably be aware of what they are and how to deal with them. A new employer is always an unknown quantity, no matter how careful you are about your research. Your old boss may have had some annoying habits, but what about your new manager? In the worst-case scenario, if you move to a new employer and recession hits, you may fall victim to the theory of 'last in, first out' and find redundancy beckoning.

Every job-seeker should be aware of these downsides. That does not mean you should avoid taking any new job. Risk is the companion of opportunity. The point is that effective career-building requires a full understanding of both the risks and opportunities in making a job change. With that understanding you can take steps to maximize the potential upsides and minimize the downsides. After all, staying where you are can be risky too if your favourite manager leaves, your skills stagnate or your own industry goes into decline.

Meeting the challenge of the job hunt

For some people the challenge of finding a new job is inevitably harder than for others. Issues such as ageism can be a problem. Job-hunters need to be realistic about the opportunities available to them. That does not mean they must accept rejection as an inevitable result. Older job-hunters just need to be more wily in their approach. You may not have considered taking temporary work as a route to a permanent job, but why not? Some employers may reject an applicant for an advertised post but be extremely keen to employ them, cashing in on the individual's years of experience, on a short-term basis.

Or so they think. Once you are in the door and doing the job it's amazing how often the employer suddenly realizes how easy and advantageous it would be to keep you there. If job-hunting is risky for the job-seeker, so it is also risky for the recruiter trying to identify the able and committed worker from amongst a pile of CVs.

Expert advice

In researching this book we have drawn not only on our own experiences, but also on those of many recruiters – individuals based inside employer organizations and those in specialist recruitment firms. We undertook a major survey of human resource (HR) professionals, recruitment consultants and line managers involved in the recruitment process. We received responses from across all business sectors and all sizes of organization.

Our survey sought opinions on issues related to CVs and covering letters. We queried the value of speculative applications and found them to be worth the effort. We found out how many recruiters used tests during the selection process and what particular factors turned them off or onto candidates during an interview. We asked about sensitive issues such as the appropriateness of asking for more money and the impact of ageism in recruitment, as well as how to combat it. The results are included in the relevant sections of this book, referred to using terms such as 'our research', 'our survey' or 'our respondents'.

In writing this book we also drew on the expertise of other recruitment experts in specialist areas. Our advice, based on our research findings, expert insights and our own experience, therefore reflects an up-to-date snapshot of the likes and dislikes of today's recruiters. All these factors together make this book a true insider's guide – *the* indispensable guide to the complete job-hunting experience – offering insights that might just help you land your ideal job.

Kickstart Tip

Scattered through the text we have boxed certain concepts, ideas or suggestions that we hope will give you new insights into old job-hunting challenges or a fresh approach to chew over.

To provide some extra magical inspiration, we have included celebrity tips from people who have built successful careers in a wide range of sectors, from industry and finance to sport and catering. We hope these will encourage anyone whose aspirational energies are flagging in the face of a stagnant career or a prolonged job search.

Above all we hope that this book will inspire you to take stock of what you want from your career. What is your ideal job? If your current working environment is failing to satisfy your needs, we hope you feel empowered to look for something more fulfilling.

Becoming a career mercenary is a worthwhile option for us all. Whatever your age or experience, you can kickstart your career.

Part I

Foundation Stages

Chapter 1

Taking Personal Stock

Successful job-hunting is equivalent to running an effective sales and marketing campaign: you are the goods on offer and you want to show them in their best light.

Kickstart Tip

Successful selling of any item is founded on a real and complete understanding of the product. How well do you really know yourself?

Are you making assumptions about where your skills lie? Have you recently reviewed your goals? Are you still certain you want the same things you wanted five years ago?

If you aren't sure, the first step in your own marketing campaign should be a period of honest self-analysis. Your should ask yourself a number of probing questions designed to clarify or reaffirm your individual career path.

In broad terms this self-analysis will consider:

- What kind of person am I?
- What do I want from my career?
- Where am I now on my career path?
- Where do I want to get to next?
- Where do I want to arrive eventually?

Dare to dream: where do you want your career to go?

No one gets what they want in life unless they know what that is. Eager job-hunters may want to sit right down, draw up their CV and send it off. If you are sure you know what job you want, go for it. But are you really sure?

Some people assume they know what they want; but when they get it, the reality is a disappointment. You were sure you wanted to become a finance director last year. Are you still sure?

Spending some time imagining what your dream career would involve now, in five years, in ten years and right up to retirement is time well spent. Dreaming without action will get you nowhere, but constructive imagining can serve several useful purposes. These can include:

- crystallizing what it is you want now;
- identifying possibilities previously ignored; and
- increasing motivation to work towards your goals.

Crystallizing what it is you want now

Our needs and wants change over time. If you started out your career wanting to become a city dealer, is that what you want now? Are you still prepared to put up with the long hours and competitive stress? Maybe you are now attracted by the idea of moving into a back-office role, or becoming more involved in areas such as staff training and management.

It's easy to get stuck in a rut. If we start our career along route A, the outside world generally expects us to carry on along route A, even when our inner voice starts questioning whether we might rather be doing something completely different. Taking a conscious decision to spend some time dreaming of what we might want allows that inner voice to come to the fore.

Identifying possibilities previously ignored

If you are unsure what it is you want from your career, then you need to give yourself free rein to imagine yourself in a wide range of different occupations. Think about everyone you know whose work ever interested you. You may unearth a past dream that still excites you. You may identify a new career option you didn't know about or didn't consider when you left college.

Increasing motivation to work towards your goals

It may be that the dream is an extension of your original chosen career path – say to be running the marketing department of a major plc in five years' time, a board director two years later and managing director five years after that. In this case, you have confirmation that you are working in the right area. Reaffirming that your existing dream is what you want can boost your motivation to deliver your best performance at work.

If your dream is to move in a totally new direction, then imagining the new you in the new workplace can give you the impetus to actually make the change. Switching directions isn't necessarily easy. You will need to persuade other people, perhaps your partner or an employer, that your intentions are serious. If the dream is exciting enough, you are more likely to have the incentive and commitment to try and make it come true.

When you are dreaming about your desired future, try to do so in a constructive way. The following suggestions may help:

- **Don't prejudge**
  Ban from your mind words such as 'can't', 'impossible' and 'never'. You can add reality into the equation later. Initially you just want to establish what you really, really want.

- **Allow yourself time**
  You need enough time to be able to explore whims and ideas at leisure.

- **Avoid situations where you are likely to be interrupted**
  Try to find a period where you won't be disturbed. If you think you might be interrupted it can be hard to let your mind focus on yourself properly.

- **Be prepared**
  Have a pen and paper handy to jot down any brainwaves.

The career-dreaming process shouldn't be a one-off exercise. Regularly focusing on your needs is a useful exercise for examining where you are going and whether you need to change direction.

A practical assessment – the career audit

While dreaming about your dream career or ideal job helps to get you motivated, at some point you have to take a realistic look at your skills and potential. Do you have what it takes to make your dream come true?

So, the next vital step in building your ideal career is to assess your current strengths and weaknesses. This self-analysis is essential for coming to a realistic assessment about whether you have a chance of achieving your desires. It may also flag up some extra skills you need to develop to make it happen.

Identifying your strengths

Your aim is to build as full a picture as possible of your own qualities. You should also try to describe your strengths wherever possible in practical terms. For example, old chestnuts such as 'good with people' or 'a good communicator' mean very little on their own.

Explain to yourself what you mean by these phrases. Are you good with people in that you are adept at building team morale? Or are you an expert listener who inspires trust in those with whom you work?

If you are a good communicator, does that mean you can explain complex processes to new employees in simple terms? Are you praised for the quality of your month-end reports on your division's performance?

This initial process of identifying your strengths and weaknesses is for your eyes only. Your aim is to create as comprehensive a list as possible. You can identify which qualities are most relevant to your chosen career path later.

To make sure you don't miss anything out, try to answer the following questions:

- What have your recent appraisals commented on?
- What have your colleagues praised you for recently?
- What has given you the most personal satisfaction recently?
- Why did you get this sense of satisfaction?
- What did your tutors/teachers praise you for in school/college?
- Do your friends complement you on anything you do well?

You can also try thinking about your skills or qualities in different areas such as:

- communication – verbal and written;
- numerical ability;
- IT skills;
- technical knowledge – in IT, finance etc.;
- decision-making;
- creativity – in thought, words, pictures, planning;
- leadership – do others follow your example?
- staff management – are you a good team-builder?
- training – explaining ideas or processes to others;
- reliability – punctuality, accuracy;

- physical fitness; or
- attitude – positive outlook, determination.

Write down every positive attribute you identify. Beside each one, make a note of examples that demonstrate how you have used this attribute in practice. The examples don't have to be taken from the workplace. They could involve situations where you have resolved family conflicts, contributed to a project at college, helped with raising funds for your local football club or proved an asset to your friends in some way.

> **Kickstart Tip**
>
> Anything that highlights your skills and abilities in a positive light is worth jotting down. You might want to use these examples later in your CV or during your job interview.

At the very least, your notes can help to keep you feeling positive about yourself as you set off on your job-hunting, career-boosting journey.

Of course, you need to identify any key weaknesses too. Are there any significant areas in your skills armoury that let you down and that might obstruct your job search? If so, ask yourself whether there are obvious solutions. Think about any training courses or extra work experience you can tap into quickly that could help strengthen your employer appeal.

Current career issues

Throughout your self-analysis process, you can gain useful insights into your needs and skills from your past employment experiences. If you are already in work, consider how well that job meets your current needs.

Ask yourself the following questions:

- What are your principal job responsibilities?
- What aspects of your job do you enjoy most?
- What aspects of your job do you enjoy least?
- Is there anything you miss about your last job?
- In what areas of your work have you been most successful?

- What do you like most about your current employer?
- Do you have any problems with your employer?
- Why are you thinking of making a career move?

You can also start thinking about how your next job could be different:

- What are you looking for in your next role?
- Is there anything you would rather avoid in your next job? Why?
- What are you looking for in your next employer?

Asking questions like these helps to formalize what you are really looking for from your next job move.

Practical planning – building the bridge to the future

Kickstart Tip

At this stage you should have:

- imagined what you want your career to be;
- assessed your potential – your strengths and weakness; and
- thought rationally about how your current job, or any past work experiences, have met your needs.

You now need to process all that information to come up with your career plan. If you are at the start of your career, this means deciding what type of role you want to fill and in what kind of organization. This is a big decision, and one you should take assisted by any careers advisory services available to you. Talk to anyone you know who is already working in the career area that attracts you.

If you are already in work, the implications are probably less dramatic. Most people emerge from their self-analysis reasonably happy with their general career choice. You may, however, have decided you want to change jobs to obtain greater variety, new opportunities for self-development or improved pay and conditions.

You still need to plan your job move carefully. A lack of proper planning will probably leave you ultimately disappointed, your career goals frustrated. A series of unplanned job moves can result in a haphazard CV and a far longer journey to reach your desired career destination.

You also need to consider what the new employer will be looking for in you, an issue we consider more fully in the next chapter.

Kickstart Tip

What makes us attractive to a potential employer is our proven ability; in other words, the things we have done before. Therefore, we have most chance of being offered new jobs that most closely resemble our old one.

As a result, successful job-hunting may require some compromise between the employer's needs and our own. We will probably be offered a job that incorporates most of the skills we demonstrated in the last job, but that builds in some new elements.

When planning your job move, it's worth thinking about the timing in terms of maximizing your strengths. Perhaps you aren't really enjoying your current job, but have only been in it for a year. Is there an advantage in staying an extra 12 months to maximize what you learn from the experience? This can be true in job roles or industry sectors with a strong seasonal element. If you complete the cycle twice you probably have a far better understanding of how it works, which means you have more value to offer a new employer.

Radical change

In some cases, the self-analysis process may have confirmed your desire for more radical change. What if you want to set out in a whole new career direction? If this is the case, you need to think carefully about the practical implications.

- **You may need to retrain.**
  Will you need to do a part-time or evening course outside work? Can you fund or obtain grants for full-time retraining?

- **Can you switch career, but stay with your employer?**
  If your employer values you, then the option to switch department may be available in order to keep your skills within the organization.

Setting goals

Once you have established or confirmed your preferred career direction, it's worth setting goals for where you want to be when. Try writing down what you want to be doing in five, ten and 15 years' time.

Your goals should be as specific as possible. Think about the following issues:

- What job role/title do I want to have?
- How much responsibility for staff do I want?
- How much do I want to be earning?

Put these goals away in a safe place so you can dig them out in future. You should establish the habit of reviewing your goals every year, updating them as your aspirations develop. If you are currently in a job, an ideal time to do this would be at the same time as your annual performance review, if you have one.

Double-checking values

As you set yourself goals, it's worth checking that they are consistent with each other and with your own internal values. Achieving high career goals may come with a price in terms of time commitment, periods away from family or friends, frequent travel or stress.

For example, if you want to be an IT consultant you may well have to spend many nights in hotel rooms away from your own home. If spending time with your family is a high priority you may be better considering a corporate IT role, rather than the consultancy option.

If you want an academic career but dream of driving a sports car, living in Mayfair and staying in the best hotels on holiday, you may find yourself frustrated with an academic's salary. Be as honest with yourself as possible.

Decisions to downshift

When considering career moves, the common assumption is that we all want to move to a more challenging, demanding, better-paid job. That may not always be the case.

You may have spent the last ten years working ever longer hours, getting overtired and missing out on family events by being kept late in the office. Are you happy to keep on doing that? As long as you can pay the bills you don't have to keep pushing up the career ladder just to meet other people's expectations.

You might want to move to a less pressurized role. Would you be more content in a less dynamic company just half an hour's drive from home rather than an hour's commute away?

Perhaps you have a young family and want to consider the potential for working part-time or building a portfolio career combining a variety of part-time roles that give you more flexibility and more control over managing your time.

These are as legitimate reasons for making a career change as the desire to earn more money or be recognized as a high-flyer by your peers.

The power of self-belief

There is no point deluding yourself if your career dream is absolutely impossible. If you want to be an astronaut but you suffer from claustrophobia and don't want to leave the UK, you'd be better off directing your dreams in more appropriate areas.

However, your ambitions may be possible but unlikely, or at least extremely challenging. You then have to decide how determined you really are. How much do you really want that dream to come true? How much effort are you prepared to put into making it happen?

If you are 100 per cent certain about what you want, and prepared to do everything you can within the bounds of law and human morality to make it happen, then your will power may just get you there.

Be warned, however, that other people who lack your sense of determination, optimism, self-belief and commitment may mock you. Be wary who you share your dreams with. Confide initially in those whose judgement you trust and who you believe will support you, rather than those who will delight in deflating your bubble for the sake of it.

> ## Kickstart Tip
>
> Whatever your course of action, aim for your optimum outcome. Even if you ultimately fall short of the bullseye, you will probably finish better off than if you start out aiming for an apparently more achievable target.

The world is full of people who have achieved their dreams; it is also full of people who had a dream but didn't bother trying to make it happen. Which group would you rather be in?

Chapter summary: key points

- Building a successful career requires you to know yourself and your dreams thoroughly.
- Give yourself time and permission to imagine different career outcomes.
- Build reality into the process by considering your strengths and weaknesses.
- Consider how well your past job(s) have suited you.
- Finish your self-analysis by drawing up your career aims in a set of specific goals.
- Remember to think of employers' needs in planning your next job move.
- Ensure your values are consistent with your career aims.
- Don't assume career success must mean more pressure and promotion. It's OK to downshift if that meets your current desires.
- Believe in yourself; will power is a valuable driver for making your career dreams come true.

Chapter **2**

Understanding the Employer

Being a successful job-hunter doesn't just require you to have a good idea about the kind of job you want; you also have to understand what employers will be wanting from you. Then you just have to persuade them that those qualities are in fact what you possess.

The balance of push and pull

When people decide to make a job move, they usually do so because of a combination of 'push' and 'pull' factors. The push could result from being sidelined, being passed over for promotion, experiencing conflict with a new line manager or the threat of redundancy. The pull relates to seeing the opportunity for new challenges, self-development and broader experience in the new role – being pulled towards better opportunities.

> ### Kickstart Tip
>
> As far as the employer is concerned, the ideal candidate is someone with no push behind their job move, someone who is doing extremely well where they are, has huge opportunities there, who is marked out as a rising star but who can see that the new employer has something slightly better to offer.

The psychology behind this is simple; it's the basic reaction of thinking that if something is in demand and valued, then it must be good. If something is being pushed out and rejected from where it is, perhaps there is something wrong with it.

While this is a simplistic scenario, job-hunters should bear it in mind throughout their job search. Play up the positive and underplay the negative reasons behind your desire to find a new role. If your employer is going bust, that's a fair enough reason to be looking to get out. But negatives that might reflect badly on you should generally be kept to yourself.

A dose of realism: what do employers look for?

When employers assess your suitability for joining them, they will be considering three key factors:

- Does your desire to work within the organization fit into a logical career plan?
- How would you add value to the organization?
- Will you fit into the team and the department?

Career logic

Your application needs to make sense in terms of fitting into a logical career plan. If it does, then that suggests the 'pull' factors are in place.

In order for your application to appear logical, you will need to demonstrate a high degree of knowledge about the organization and its activities, including its sector and competitors. If you can't do this, how can you have made a logical career decision that you would like to work there?

You must also show genuine interest in the particular organization's activities. How convincingly you can do this is partly determined by what you have done before. This means that in the early years of your career you should find you can move around between sectors, but once you pick up significant long-term experience in one area, your options will close in. If you have spent 20 years in marketing for arts organizations and suddenly wish to switch to insurance, questions will be asked about how genuinely interested you are in the financial services sector.

Career history aside, raw enthusiasm is very attractive to employers. The basic signals you give in your written communication, your speech and body language can reinforce your appeal or leave a lacklustre impression. Energy is appealing; apathy isn't.

Adding value to the organization

Employers want people who will add value to the organization. This must always be the focus of your application. How can you, as an individual, improve the performance of the organization you seek to join?

There may be an element of technical proficiency involved here. Do you have the required skill level necessary to fulfil a certain role well? This is clearly an essential basic requirement.

In addition, softer skills are increasingly important. Although there are still some roles where the primary requirement is technical ability – being a backroom expert – the majority of modern roles require high levels of interaction with other individuals inside and outside the organization. The spread of open-plan offices has increased the importance of simply being able to get along with other people.

Employers are increasingly interested in issues such as:

- How well do you communicate verbally and in writing with other people?
- How good are you at influencing others – inside and outside the organization?
- How effective are you at sharing the knowledge you have?
- How skilled are you at planning a project involving people at a range of levels?
- How effective are you at taking that project through to completion, on time and on budget?

Many of these skills can be summarized by the term 'team player'. You won't do yourself any harm if you persuade employers that you are this kind of person.

Leadership ability is also in demand. Again this requires effective communication and influencing skills, as well as vision, the ability to make decisions and the courage to stand up and be counted.

Kickstart Tip

When applying to any organization, try to think in terms of how the package of skills you offer can be turned to its advantage. What do you have that someone else doesn't? It could be:

- knowledge of competitors;
- knowledge of transferable techniques from similar sectors;
- acknowledged creative insight; or
- unrivalled energy and enthusiasm.

Fitting in

You need your prospective employer to believe that you would fit well within the department or the particular team you would be joining. This partly involves demonstrating that the ways you can add value, as described above, will complement the current skills and abilities displayed by the existing team members.

In addition the recruiter will be seeking reassurance that your outlook and working methods will fit well with the departmental style and the particular approach of your potential line manager or senior management colleagues.

Other factors

Some employers may be interested in individuals with a Master of Business Administration (MBA) qualification, although this is not necessarily the case and there is certainly a pecking order in terms of how well individual business schools are perceived. An MBA from one of the famous top UK, European or US schools (such as London Business School, INSEAD in France or Harvard in the USA) is most likely to impress. Although MBAs won't necessarily guarantee you make it to an interview shortlist, they can sometimes help you change direction slightly or give you access to a valuable alumni network that you can call on to good effect later in your career. As we discuss in Chapter 11, Making Your Own Opportunities, effective networking can be the most effective way to boost your career.

Depending on your sector, international experience may also be an attractive element on a candidate's CV. Although the UK remains perhaps more insular than many other economies in terms of recruiting globally, the UK's leading businesses are becoming increasingly global in their operations.

> ### Kickstart Tip
>
> If you have gained useful experience working overseas, preferably in an advanced economy, you will almost certainly become more attractive to employers.

US or continental European experience tends to be more highly valued than Third World exposure, although this will again vary by sector; in the charity or not-for-profit sectors, time spent in a poor economy could make you more attractive than work experience in the USA. As a general rule, work experience overseas is far more likely to increase your appeal than reduce it.

Selling yourself

When you think in terms of what you can offer the employer, you are developing the mindset that will enable you to sell yourself effectively. This is important at each stage of any job application.

> ### Kickstart Tip
>
> **Whether applying to an advertised vacancy, talking to a recruitment consultant, writing a speculative letter to a target employer, drafting your CV or attending a job interview, your focus must always be:** *this is what I can do for you.*

Privately, in your own mind, you will obviously be asking yourself, what can this employer do for me? Does it fit with my personal career needs? Is its style of working, its cultural character a good fit with mine? You might even start to discuss such issues at a later interview stage or, preferably, after you have been offered a job and are considering whether or not you want to accept. However, for all public purposes until that point, you talk only about adding value to the organization.

Your best opportunity to sell yourself really comes at the interview stage of the recruitment process. This is also when the recruiter will form an opinion of your real suitability for the organization. Therefore, our research questionnaire asked headhunters, HR professionals and line managers to rate a number of factors in terms of their importance for influencing their decision during an interview.

Enthusiasm for the job emerged as the highest-rated factor in influencing the recruiter's decision – mentioned by 85 per cent of our survey respondents. Overall, the top ten key factors in order of importance were found to be:

- enthusiasm for the job;
- communication skills;
- ability to fit into a team;
- punctuality when attending the interview;

- evidence of appropriate attitudes and behaviour;
- relevance of experience;
- eye contact;
- personal chemistry and rapport;
- evidence of an understanding of the position; and
- appearance.

We look in detail at how you should try to maximize the impact of your interview performance in Chapter 13, Interview Savvy and Chapter 14, Tackling Frequently Asked Interview Questions.

Ageism

Depending on the kind of position you are looking for, age and experience can be an advantage, or it can make the job search that much harder. Our research tried to find out when ageism can kick into the recruitment process. Many people believe that ageism doesn't start to have an impact until the age of 50. However, the largest proportion of respondents to our questionnaire said they considered candidates become subject to ageism in recruitment at the age of 40, while a quite significant group thought ageism had an effect by the age of 35. One in ten said that age issues depended on the job, the employing organization or the responsibilities involved.

Generally speaking, things may be tougher for most job-hunters over 40, but there are things you can do to maximize your appeal and minimize the age issue.

Kickstart Tip

According to our research, the best line of attack for candidates worried about ageism is to emphasize their experience; this means clearly demonstrating, with objective examples, how you have added value to other organizations and therefore how you could add value to your target employer.

Many of the tips for overcoming ageism focus on the individual's attitude – never giving up, never 'thinking old', presenting yourself positively, demonstrating your adaptability, selling yourself on your skills and showing yourself comfortable with change.

Overall, the most frequent suggestions for combating ageism include:

- clearly demonstrating the value of your experience;
- being flexible, open to change and willing to learn;
- emphasizing your enthusiasm and energy;
- undertaking continued professional development;
- demonstrating a positive, confident outlook;
- reviewing your style of dress or general appearance;
- keeping fit and looking healthy; and
- keeping up with technology, particularly ensuring computer literacy.

The emphasis is on you to overcome any suspected ageism you encounter. Only 5 per cent of our survey respondents said they thought that it was up to employers to change their attitudes. The bottom line is that supply and demand applies to the recruitment market as to any other. Employers determine what it is they demand, in terms of skills and personal qualities. They will then generally seek to find the closest match from the supply of skills and services available. Your responsibility is to present yourself in the best light, to boost yourself up the demand scale by virtue of your breadth of experience, depth of knowledge and any other advantages that age gives you over some younger gun.

You can also act tactically to tip the scales in your favour. As a general rule, you should avoid showing prominently at the top of your CV anything that might put the recruiter off. This may include your age if you are over 40. If you simply state your age at the top of page one, as is common practice, you may find your application jettisoned into the reject pile without the recruiter's eye straying down the page to even look at the skills you have to offer.

Such behaviour has led some people to suggest that anyone worried about encountering ageism should omit their age completely from their CV. However, this is not our recommended approach, since you are actually making an issue of your age by the very fact that you are leaving it out.

A better tactic is simply to include your age at the bottom of the last page of your CV. In this way the recruiter should have already looked through your career history and been impressed by your experience by the time your age is discovered. This approach maximizes your appeal and tempts the recruiter to find out more about the added value you could bring at a face-to-face interview.

Kickstart Tip

Perhaps the best way of all for the older job-hunter to overcome ageism is to make good use of the network you have built up over your lifetime. Theoretically, the older you are, the larger your network, and potentially the more senior and influential the people contained within it.

Using any and all of your contacts effectively is undoubtedly your best bet for finding fulfilling work. We look more closely at how to go about this in Chapter 11, Making Your Own Opportunities.

If you feel you are suffering from ageism during your job search, you might get useful advice and encouragement from the Campaign Against Age Discrimination in Employment, whose contact details are included in the Appendix.

Other forms of discrimination

Ageism isn't the only barrier to success that exists in the workplace. Sexism, racism and prejudice against the disabled can also, unfortunately, sometimes hinder talented individuals' chances of landing their ideal job or building the kind of career they want. Obviously, discrimination is illegal under the Sex Discrimination Act, the Race Relations Act and the Disability Discrimination Act. Employers found to have breached anti-discrimination legislation can face hefty compensation payouts awarded against them by employment tribunals.

However, proving discrimination has occurred can be extremely difficult, as well as being emotionally tough for the individual concerned. Campaigning organizations, such as the Equal Opportunities Commission, the Commission for Racial Equality and the Disability Rights Commission, may be able to offer help and support for people who feel they are encountering discrimination in the workplace. Their contact details are included in the Appendix.

One major problem with discrimination is that physical or real barriers to success do not need to exist for an individual's career path still to be impeded. The existence of so-called glass ceilings that stop women making it to the very top of the career ladder have long been debated in the employment world. There is little doubt that some sectors and some employers have better records than others in supporting women in the workforce and their career development.

Sectors with particularly macho images – such as the City of London or the surgery discipline within the medical profession – will undoubtedly be tougher environments for women than others with a higher, longer established female representation at senior levels – such as the media, the teaching profession, human resources and public relations.

As an individual, there is relatively little you can do alone to improve the situation. Changing the world and the workplace takes time and force of numbers.

What you can do is try to find out about the culture of the workplace in your target career or potential employer before you are committed to working there. Some companies are trying to become more meritocratic or actively pursuing diversity programmes. For example, in 1997 women made up just 11 per cent of the 800 managers at global food and consumer products company Sara Lee; by 2001 that proportion had increased to around 21 per cent. Research to identify the best employers is conducted fairly regularly, and it's worth trying to minimize your chances of running up against hostile environments if you can. There are also reference books that can help you, such as *Britain's Top Employers: A Guide to the Best Companies to Work For*, published by the Corporate Research Foundation, which tries to give an indication of the cultures and styles of the companies included.

You can also make a point of joining any work-related or professional groups that represent your interests. Women in many professions can now join women's groups that enable them to support each other and share experiences. Racially based groups tend to be less common or to have a less high profile, but they do exist. Apart from the mutual support available, such groups can provide excellent networking opportunities – an activity of great value, whether or not you are concerned about glass ceilings or discrimination.

In general, as you progress through your career, take any steps you can to minimize the risk of discrimination. This advice applies to anyone, of any gender, ethnic background or disability level. You should:

- always do the best work you can;
- treat others – whether in more senior or more junior levels – with the same degree of respect that you would expect them to show to you;

- try not to make an issue of your own 'difference';
- accept that you should make an effort to fit into the prevailing culture, although this shouldn't mean abandoning your personal beliefs or principles;
- highlight your abilities and achievements whenever appropriate – false modesty won't help you to win respect or promotion;
- identify any supportive colleagues or more senior personnel who can become your allies in the workplace; and
- be prepared to stand up for yourself if you believe you have been treated unfairly.

Chapter summary: key points

- Employers are more interested in candidates who are motivated by the pull of new opportunities than by those pushed out into the job market.
- Try to ensure that working for your target employer appears logical in the context of your career plan.
- Employers are highly attracted by new employees who can clearly add value to the organization through their skills and experience.
- Team-working and softer skills are as important as technical or intellectual ability.
- MBAs can have some value, but pick a quality business school.
- Overseas work experience is generally attractive to employers.
- Be prepared to sell yourself in terms of 'this is what I can do for you'.
- Enthusiasm is one of the most important attributes you can demonstrate when you get to the interview stage.
- Ageism does exist in the job market; your best approach for overcoming it is to express your skills, experience, flexibility and enthusiasm, rather than leaving your age off your CV.
- Other forms of discrimination – such as gender, race or disability – may exist.
- Do any research you can to avoid employers with poor track records in such areas.
- Network with any support groups who may be able to help you overcome the risk of discrimination.
- Be prepared to stand up for your rights if necessary.

Chapter 3

Planning an Effective Job Search

How you plan your job search will inevitably depend on a number of factors, such as the seniority of the role you seek and how widely such positions are available. Your strategy may also be affected by the urgency with which you want to find a new job. If you want to move fast, you may be wise to combine several different methods.

Varieties of job-hunting

Once you decide to kickstart your career by embarking on a new job-hunting adventure, there are a number of different routes you can decide to follow. You could:

- respond to advertised vacancies;
- register with a recruitment consultancy; and/or
- make your own speculative approaches to targeted employers.

These are not mutually exclusive options and if you are serious about finding a new position, then you may well want to undertake a three-pronged attack on the job market. However, your likely success in applying each approach will be affected by your seniority:

- Junior positions are particularly likely to be advertised in the local press and filled by local recruitment consultancies. As you progress in your career, relevant positions are more likely to be handled by specialist recruitment consultancies or to be filled by national advertising.
- At executive level, the general rule is that the more senior the position you seek, the less likely you are to find it by looking through the job ads or by registering with a recruitment consultancy. Top level positions are most likely to be filled by headhunters, or as the result of personal contacts or recommendations.

We look in detail at how to follow each route effectively later. Chapter 8, Advertised Openings considers how best to respond to advertised vacancies; Chapter 10, Making the Most of Recruitment Consultancies looks at making the most of the services of specialist recruiting firms, including how to catch the headhunter's eye; and Chapter

11, Making Your Own Opportunities and Chapter 12, Speculative Approaches focus on how to generate your own openings through effective speculative approaches to potential employers that you identify yourself.

A numbers game

As you set out on your search for your dream job, remember that job-hunting is a numbers game. An advertised vacancy for a managerial position might generate up to 100 responses. Of these, 12 applicants may be invited to a first-round interview with the recruitment consultant. Four or five might then be shortlisted, and just two or three will generally be invited back for a final interview. A job offer will be made to one of these remaining contenders.

On the basis of these numbers, when you respond to the job advert you have about a one in eight chance of being invited for an initial interview. Those are pretty good odds. So at this early stage, when you are spending time tailoring your CV to meet the job description, remind yourself that this is time well spent.

Don't dwell on the thought that there are 99 other applicants out there and that, theoretically, the odds are one in 100 that you are the person who will ultimately be offered the job. Focus on the one in eight. Once you get that initial interview, focus your attention on getting through to the next stage – winning a second-round interview – which has perhaps a one in two or one in three chance.

> ### Kickstart Tip
>
> Breaking the job-hunting process down in this way can make it seem less daunting, and encourages you to put all your effort and energy into doing what needs to be done to move on to the next round.

Key stages in the job hunt

Whichever job-hunting route you decide to follow, there are a number of common key stages. Each involves distinct aims for the ambitious job-hunter.

Stage 1: Researching your job market

There is no substitute for this upfront research, which can be extremely wide-ranging.

You need to research yourself – your aims and abilities – to make sure you are heading in the right direction, as we discussed in Chapter 1, Taking Personal Stock. You also need to understand the job market. What are employers looking for and how can you meet their needs? Where are the best openings for you likely to be? These issues are addressed in Chapter 2, Understanding the Employer and Chapter 5, Powerful Preparation.

The result of all this research may be a well-prepared application in response to a job advertisement or a speculative approach to a potential employer to see whether they may have a need for your services. Whatever your route, your aim in doing this research is to make sure your application is focused and realistic, and therefore more likely to succeed.

Stage 2: Winning an interview

Whether you are responding to an advert, trying to interest a recruitment consultancy in placing your skills or making an unsolicited approach to a target employer, your key aim is to obtain a face-to-face meeting.

For an advertised role, this will be a first-round interview. With a consultancy, it may be a screening or introductory assessment. After a speculative approach, it could be a meeting to discuss any potential ways in which your skills and experience could add value to the target organization. The tools that you use to win that interview might include your exploratory phone call, your CV, your completed application form or your covering letter. We consider how to make the best use of these in Chapter 6, Preparing Your Marketing Material and Chapter 12, Speculative Approaches. However, it is worth stressing that when preparing your CV or writing your covering letter, your attention should be focused on stimulating sufficient interest in the recruiter's mind so that you are invited for interview. Your aim at this stage is *not* to get the job. You may not, in the end, even want this job or want to be offered a role with this organization. However, you want the option – you want to be given the choice.

Stage 3: Winning a final-round interview

If you are invited for an initial interview, your goal then becomes winning a second-round interview. This might sometimes be the last stage of the selection process, although you are more likely to find that the second round is followed by a third and final interview.

Reaching the final-interview stage means you really are in with a good chance of winning the job offer, since by that stage you are probably one of two or three remaining candidates.

Your performance in earlier stage interviews clearly holds the key to reaching this last lap of the job hunt. Tips for mastering the interview are addressed in detail in Chapter 13, Interview Savvy and Chapter 14, Tackling Frequently Asked Interview Questions.

Stage 4: Winning a job offer

Once you have made it to the last lap and been invited back for a final-round interview, you again apply the effective interview techniques you have already demonstrated. At this stage you need to focus not only on reinforcing the recruiter's belief in your suitability for the vacant role, but also on emphasizing your enthusiasm for it. You leave no room for doubt about your willingness to accept the position if it is finally offered to you.

This doesn't mean you will actually accept the job, if you receive the offer. You will later calmly and privately assess whether this really is the job for you. But while in the interview, you entertain no such doubts.

Other potential elements of the recruitment process

Some organizations may add extra stages involving assessment centres and tests, designed to obtain objective evidence about a candidate's suitability for the vacant role. These tests can assess practical managerial skills, verbal and numerical reasoning and personality. Your aim in attending such stages is clear: do your best to make sure you are considered competent for the job. We look at how to cope with tests and assessment centres in more detail in Chapter 15, Passing the Tests.

Managing the process while in employment

Those seeking a new job while already employed need to be respectful of their current employer. This means not abusing office hours for running your job search. In any case, if you want your job search to remain private you should be extremely careful about using your current employer's email system for sending off your CV in answer to job advertisements. Many organizations have email screening systems that look out for email messages containing certain words, such as 'career' or 'job'. These messages will be automatically intercepted and read.

Your job search should therefore ideally be conducted from a PC located outside the office – most probably at home – where possible.

You should also be careful about the people you tell about your job search. You may naturally feel the need to confide in someone, but avoid the office gossip! The fewer the people who know, the better.

Public sector variations

Some people planning their next career move may contemplate moving between the private and public sectors. In fact, such crossing over is becoming increasingly common. Government initiatives in recent years have tended to encourage greater private sector involvement in formerly public sector areas, such as transport or health. There has also been a steady increase in organizations resourced by a combination of public funding and private sector investment. The blurring of traditional public/private sector boundaries in this way means that increasing numbers of people are likely to encounter public sector recruiting techniques at some stage in their career. However, there are some distinct differences between the recruitment processes applied in the private and public sectors.

In the private sector there is likely to be:

- more use of CVs;
- more one-on-one interviewing; and
- less focus on issues such as meeting target ratios related to the gender or race of staff employed.

In the public sector there will be:

- greater use of standard application forms;
- more use of panel interviews; and
- greater concern about equal opportunity issues.

As interaction between public and private sector organizations continues in future, it is likely that public sector recruiting techniques will become more widespread. Those people familiar with the private sector approach should make sure they understand the differences and how to respond to them.

Application forms

Job-hunters often find application forms extremely off-putting. In one recruitment assignment for a government department, 70 per cent of all the application forms sent out in response to enquiries were not returned. This means that, by putting in the effort to complete such a form, you are already putting yourself in with a chance that less determined people deny themselves.

The forms seem daunting because they can be long (four pages upwards) and require detailed answers to questions focused around the job specification and your experience. Don't think that you can sidestep the form and still have your application taken seriously. You should answer the form as completely as possible.

Kickstart Tip

Don't be lazy and keep writing in 'See CV' in box after box. If you do this, you won't stand a chance of being invited for an interview. Organizations that use application forms do so because they see them as the best tools for capturing the information they require for the recruitment process and for levelling the playing field between applicants.

We consider techniques for completing application forms effectively in Chapter 6, Preparing Your Marketing Material.

Panel interviews

Panel interviews are extremely common in the public sector, where appointments are often made by a selection committee. You could easily find yourself being interviewed by groups of three people upwards, perhaps even 20 or so. The interview panel will have a chairperson, but questions could be fired at you from any member. It is therefore worth finding out exactly who is on the selection panel before you arrive for your interview. Address your responses primarily to the person who asked the question, but try to make eye contact with every member of the panel. Make an effort to establish rapport with each one if you can.

Do not make assumptions about who the important individuals are. It has been known for interview candidates to ignore any women sitting on the interview panel or those people who ask no questions or make no comment. This is a stupid mistake; these may in fact be the people who have most influence over the appointment decision. You must therefore try to include everyone in the debate, even just by means of establishing eye contact.

On the other hand, be prepared for the fact that these panel sessions may sometimes be short on the social graces extended to the interviewees; sometimes candidates are not even given a formal welcome by the chairperson. Try not to let such things throw you off your stride.

Given that the interview panel involves numerous people, it is common for public sector organizations to require all shortlisted candidates to turn up for their interviews on the same day. Sometimes this may involve you meeting the other candidates on the way in or out of your interview. There may even be a dinner with the selection panel the night before the interview day, where you, and the other shortlisted candidates, will be rotated round the table to enable you to talk to as many members of the selection panel as possible.

Equal opportunity issues

Public sector organizations tend to pay more attention to equal opportunity issues during the selection process. This is partly a reflection of public sector culture, as well as a result of regulation. Under the Race Relations Act, for example, certain public bodies are subject to a general duty to promote racial equality.

As a result, you may find that you are asked to complete a monitoring form at the same time as your application form. This asks for information about your gender, any disabilities and racial origins. Although there is no legal requirement to collect this data, there is no harm in your completing it and it does provide employers with information that can help them assess whether they are achieving diversity among their employees. The monitoring form is generally separated from the main application form on receipt by the organization, but the data contained in it does help them to monitor whether they are attracting applications from a cross section of society.

The equal opportunity focus is designed to ensure that the best person for the job gets the job. This is why completing application forms thoroughly is so important. In order to ensure impartiality in the recruitment process, shortlists of interview candidates will often be drawn up on the basis of the number of features of the job specification (which could contain as many as 30 or 40 elements) they have demonstrated they meet in their application form.

Kickstart Tip

The public sector selection process will often be achieved using a matrix format, where candidates' names appear along one side and each element of the job specification along the other. To be invited for an interview you need to get as many ticks against your name as possible.

People used to the CV-style approach, where you have maximum creative freedom in shaping your sales pitch, may consider this public sector tick-in-box approach as overly bureaucratic and restrictive. However, remember that the approach aims to level the playing field between candidates; comparing each applicant on an equal basis against clearly specified criteria is seen by its advocates as extremely rigorous and fair. You must play by their rules.

Maximizing your chances in public sector recruitment

> ### Kickstart Tip
>
> Surprisingly high numbers of applicants to public sector jobs fail to do one simple thing that can significantly help their chances of success: they don't bother requesting the information or briefing pack often referred to in the job advertisement.

Don't make this mistake yourself. The briefing pack will often include huge amounts of relevant information that you can use, first to decide whether you think this job might be for you, and second to help shape your formal application. The quality of such packs can vary from simple photocopies of documents to glossy brochures. However, their contents could include:

- an annual report;
- the organization's vision or mission statement;
- the organizational structure;
- a detailed job description;
- a specification of the type of person required for the role;
- a letter from the person to whom the applicant would report in the role;
- remuneration details;
- an application form; and
- instructions for how to respond.

This information is worth its weight in gold. It tells you huge amounts about the organization, saving you your own research time. It gives you a clear idea of whether you might be suited and which of your skills and characteristics you should highlight in your application.

Once you have this information you should be well equipped to produce a comprehensive application, one that addresses every area in the person specification.

Hamish Davidson, Partner and Head of the UK Executive Search and Selection Division at PricewaterhouseCoopers, a top public sector headhunter and the man who found American Bob Kiley to run London Underground, offers some final advice for anyone applying for a public sector role:

The public sector typically expects candidates to submit a *much more compre-hensive* application than is required in the private sector. You should even try to go beyond the criteria in the person specification. In your covering letter, say why you are interested in this role. Don't just supply a two-dimensional application; you should try to create the impression of a three-dimensional person to make me want to see you.

Seasonal variations

If you are made redundant or your employer goes through a reorganization that leaves your role uncertain, you may have no control over when you start your job search. However, if you do have control, it may be worth timing your actions to fit in with the seasonal fluctuations in recruiting activity.

There are definite peaks during the year. Spring and early summer tend to be active recruiting seasons, followed by a slump in the height of summer. Recruiting activity picks up again in the autumn and generally continues through to early December.

These fluctuations are driven both by job-hunters and recruiters. There is no doubt that many people start looking for a new job after they have had a chance to relax on summer holiday and review their career options away from the hubbub of normal life. Fortunately, companies also tend to be geared up for recruiting at that time.

Of course, vacancies can occur at any time of the year. If you happen to be scanning job adverts in July or August and see something that's perfect for you, the good news is that the response rate will typically be much lower than if the ad had appeared in September or October: your reply might be one among 30 or 40 rather than one among 100. The numbers game then could really work to your advantage.

Chapter summary: key points

- To increase the effectiveness of your job search it is important to use a combination of approaches – responding to advertised vacancies, registering with a recruitment consultancy, making speculative approaches and networking personal contacts.
- Don't worry about the numbers of people who respond to adverts.
- At each stage of the job-hunting process, focus your attention on what you need to do to proceed to the next stage.

- Be subtle if you are managing your job search from your existing workplace.
- If you are applying for a role in the public sector, be aware of the characteristics of the recruiting process.
- The public sector is more likely to require you to complete a detailed application form and to attend a panel interview, and will be particularly concerned about equal opportunity issues.
- Make sure you get hold of any information or briefing packs associated with the public sector vacancy.
- You must complete the application form thoroughly if you are to stand any chance of being invited for an interview; you must demonstrate how you meet every requirement of the job or person specification.
- When attending a panel interview, do not ignore any members of the panel.
- Consider whether you want to time your job search to fit in with seasonal variations in recruitment demand.

Chapter 4

Positive Approaches

Finding the right job for your next career move can take longer than you would like. If you are job-hunting while currently employed, the frustration is at least eased by the fact that you are still earning money. Those out of work face a tougher psychological challenge to keep motivated and maintain a positive outlook.

Redundancy

The toughest psychological challenge of all faces those going through redundancy. Cary Cooper, BUPA Professor of Organizational Psychology and Health at UMIST, says that people who are made redundant *suffer*, no matter how much publicity is given to the fact that they have lost their jobs because of a financial downturn or industrial decline rather than because of anything they have done individually. 'These people still feel rejected,' he says. 'Even if rationally they should be saying, "I'm not the only one, there are other people made redundant and it's because the business is in decline", they still psychologically feel they are responsible and they feel rejected. They feel bad.'

The news of redundancy can mark the start of an emotional roller coaster. People not expecting the news inevitably experience an initial shock and a sense of loss. After that, some people may actually experience a feeling of elation and enter a period when they throw themselves into looking for a new job, full of energy and optimism. If they find one quickly, all well and good. But if they don't, another emotional plunge may be on the way: it's hard not to start worrying about whether you will ever work again and how you will pay the bills when the redundancy money starts to run out.

Kickstart Tip

Trying to kickstart your career after being made redundant can be hard work – psychologically as well as in the ordinary job-hunting sense. A series of highs and lows is normal and to be expected. If you find yourself in this situation, try not to be too hard on yourself.

However, there are a number of simple things you can do to try and keep yourself on the right track and minimize the roller coaster effect. You should:

- establish a daily routine;
- follow a structured job-hunting process as described throughout this book; and
- use any psychological trick you can think of to keep yourself positive.

Establishing a routine

Routine is your ally in the job-hunting process. If you have no current job, you need to establish a regular pattern for your daily activities. 'The routine you should follow is that of a normal working day,' says Professor Cooper. 'If you used to start work at nine, after you have been made redundant you should still get up and start your job-hunting at 9 o'clock.'

You can, of course, build some flexibility into the regime. A former director of a major UK listed company found himself unexpectedly made redundant. He was used to an orderly, office, working life, so he followed expert advice and established his own job-hunting routine. From Monday to Thursday from 8.30 a.m. to 5.30 p.m. he treated his search for a new job as a full-time activity. He treated Friday as a bonus day off, and enjoyed normal relaxed weekends.

The advantage of establishing a regular pattern is that it helps to keep your momentum going. You don't waste time and emotional energy thinking you ought to be getting on with your job search; you just do it.

> ### Kickstart Tip
>
> Establishing a strict routine also helps those around you to take your job-searching intentions seriously. What you don't want to do is to get sucked into using your time at home for doing a random selection of odd jobs. Maintain a clear division between the time you spend working – that is, finding a new job – and your free time, when you can decide to paint the spare room if you wish.

If you manage your time effectively, you can expect to spend less time out of work. The length of your job search should be inversely proportional to the share of each day you devote to it, and the number of avenues you pursue.

When establishing your routine, ideally you need to establish a space where you carry out your job-searching activity – a study, spare bedroom or corner of the living room where you can set up your personal office, keep your job-hunting notes and preferably be undisturbed by other family members.

Following a structured job-hunting process

You may have been forced into your job search by a redundancy notice, but you can still take the opportunity to try to land a new, better job – maybe even your ideal job. Perhaps redundancy will prove to be the trigger that will enable you to kickstart your career.

The reason for your job search does not change the fundamental points we make throughout this book. If you are to maximize the outcome of your job search, you need to follow a highly structured approach. As we said in Chapter 1, Taking Personal Stock, you should:

- write down your career dreams;
- assess your strengths and abilities; and
- clarify your aims – what kind of job do you want, in what sector?

You don't necessarily want just to find another job exactly the same as the one you have been doing. If your sector is in decline, you could find yourself going through redundancy all over again in a few years' time.

Once you have defined your desired job, or a number of jobs that would meet your criteria, make sure you identify all the possible sources for finding those openings. Don't forget to consider:

- advertised vacancies – discussed in Chapter 8, Advertised Openings;
- recruitment consultancies – considered in Chapter 10, Making the Most of Recruitment Consultancies;
- identifying working opportunities for yourself – as discussed in Chapter 11, Making Your Own Opportunities and Chapter 12, Speculative Approaches. Making the most of your personal network is a key element of this process and one of the best ways for finding new work.

Psychological tricks

No one would say that finding a new job when you are out of work is anything but a tough psychological experience. You need to be prepared for that. As Professor Cooper says: 'You have to acknowledge that you will be rejected. In fact, the more proactive you are, the more rejection letters you are likely to receive. But you need to keep active, keep to a routine and keep positive.'

You might find you need to use some simple psychological tricks to keep your motivation up. You might for example:

- write down your key job-hunting goals and refer to them regularly;
- consider sticking your key goals on the wall in the room where you base your job-hunting work;
- use your imagination to create positive images of yourself. For example, if you feel your motivation slipping, close your eyes and picture yourself picking up a letter from the doormat, opening it and reading the words 'I am pleased to offer you a position . . .' Imagine your feelings at that moment – the excitement, the thrill of success;
- use stimuli to get your motor running again if you find you start to flag at a particular point of the day. Is there some music you can play that boosts your energy? Perhaps you could take some exercise at this point – even just a brisk half-hour walk. Exercise in itself can help you to maintain a positive outlook as a result of the feel-good hormones – endorphins – released in the body;
- at the end of each day, write down the first thing you will do next morning so that you have an immediate task to complete when you start the day's job-searching work; and
- make a point of speaking regularly to all the positive, supportive people you know and try to avoid those of a more negative nature.

There may be some particular aspects of the job-hunting process you find hardest. If so, try to devise strategies that make them easier for you to complete. Think rationally about why they cause you problems.

For example, you might be the kind of personality who is daunted at the thought of calling up someone you don't know well, or at all, and talking to them about career opportunities. You may, as a result, put off taking action that could be bringing you nearer to finding the job you want.

Don't be defeated. Think about the worse thing that could go wrong. If you call someone you don't know and the call goes badly, what would the worst result be? Well, the call could result in no work, no leads and no help in your job search. The worst thing that could happen is that the person who was a complete stranger to you two minutes ago is still a complete stranger after you put the phone down.

On the other hand, you have nothing to lose and everything to gain by making that call. This could be the one person who leads you to your ideal job.

Outplacement services

Although the modern psychological contract between employer and employee means that the individual must take responsibility for managing their own career development, redundancy can still prick some employers' consciences. In addition, employers know that laying off some staff can upset those employees who remain behind; the people still in work can become worried about their own job security and become disenchanted with the employer, particularly if they feel that those made redundant have been treated badly.

As a result, some employers see it as being in their own best interests to engage the services of an outplacement firm to offer expert advice and job-hunting resources to help their redundant employees find new jobs. This can be the case whether large numbers of people are being laid off in one go, or whether a single senior executive has been forced to leave.

What is outplacement?

Most people, unless they have been made redundant themselves, will not generally come across outplacement specialists. Outplacement simply means the process of advising individuals on how best to go about finding a new job and helping them with the different stages in the process. It does not mean specifically finding actual job openings or acting as a recruitment consultant. The nature of outplacement services varies hugely, depending on the particular circumstances. For example, if a group of workers are being made redundant, the employer may buy in a packaged service, at a fixed fee per head, which will enable the redundant staff to use specific services for a limited period of time. After that period, perhaps three months, they will be on their own.

Such group packages could typically include group seminars on topics such as:

- identifying your skills;
- understanding the job market;
- preparing a CV;
- completing application forms;
- effective letter-writing;
- interview preparation; and
- managing the job search.

Outplacement firms will generally provide a manual summarizing their key advice and containing samples of CVs and letters. They will also generally provide resources – office space, reference material, job-vacancy databases, computer and Internet access or typing services – to help people manage their job search. There may also be one-to-one counselling sessions with a consultant to talk about your own particular needs and how to go about an effective job search. Hazel Bunston, a consultant at outplacement firm Penna Sanders & Sidney, says:

> The hardest part of outplacement is self-awareness and having an idea of where you 'fit in'. Once people are out of work there is a tendency to apply for jobs in a spray-gun fashion, or even accept jobs which are not completely right, for fear of not finding an alternative. You should always approach redundancy as a career move and not be panicked into making hasty decisions. Use the redundancy payoff for what it is: a fighting fund that will give you time and space to find the right career.

Personalized, face-to-face advice generally becomes more extensive the more senior the individual being helped by the outplacement firm and the more expensive the services bought for them by their former employer. At the top end of the spectrum, most likely where an extremely senior individual has had to leave the organization (perhaps its chief executive or another senior director), the outplacement services paid for by the employer may be open-ended, offering the executive personalized support and advice for as long as it takes to find them new employment. The services offered may include input from psychologists, personalized career plans and introductions to headhunter and venture capital contacts.

Tony May, a founder partner of career strategy consultants Stork & May, which handles top-end outplacement assignments, says:

We have regular headhunter lunches. We know the key individuals, the sectors they operate in and the kind of assignments they are handling. We also have good networks with private equity firms and we know about non-executive directorships and interim management roles; we know the key players in those markets.

Outplacement firms at the top end of the market can also offer particular help to high-profile individuals whose reputations have suffered a mauling in the press, advising them on how likely they are to find another high-profile role or whether they need to think about other options, such as investing in other people's businesses. Stork & May's success is based upon their extensive range of industry and personal contacts and the amount of consultant time they dedicate to each individual. Services at this level don't come cheap; the charge to employers for open-ended, personalized, full support for a single senior executive could cost from around £30,000 upwards.

Making the most of outplacement

If you are offered outplacement services by your former employer, and if you have the chance to influence the choice of provider or whether to take the services at all, check exactly what is being offered to you. How much personal advice will you get? Can you ring up the outplacement consultant for a chat whenever you like? For how long will you be able to make use of the outplacement firm's resources? Are these services really of value to you?

The more senior you are, the greater the likelihood that you will be able to influence the choice of outplacement firm. In this case, you should try to talk to and visit a number of different firms to find out what they offer you and at what price.

Kickstart Tip

You may want to negotiate the terms of your severance package so that you can use a more expensive outplacement firm and take a slightly smaller cash payout, or vice versa. If you are not offered outplacement services as part of your severance package, you may want to consider approaching an outplacement firm directly yourself.

Not all firms will act for individuals who approach them directly, but some do. Their fees will probably be slightly less than they would charge a corporate client, but they will still be significant, so you need to be certain that you will be getting value for money. Make sure you find out all about the services offered, and the firm's track record, before you make your decision.

Chapter summary: key points

- Job-hunting after being made redundant can be a tough psychological experience, so you need to be prepared for the inevitable emotional roller coaster.
- Treat your job search as if it were a job itself.
- Establish a daily routine for your job-hunting activity and don't be sidetracked into doing odd jobs around the house.
- Follow the recommended job-hunting stages: identifying your aims and abilities and applying the job-hunting methods most likely to generate results.
- Use any psychological tricks you can to maintain a positive outlook, including visualizing yourself being successful and making a point of staying in regular touch with positive-minded people.
- If you have access to outplacement services, make the most of what is offered for however long the services are available to you.
- If you have any influence over the choice of outplacement firm, find out exactly what services are available, for how long and at what price; try to find as personalized a service as possible.
- Consider including outplacement provision in your severance package negotiations.

Chapter 5

Powerful Preparation

You can't cheat in the job-hunting game, not unless you are either extremely lucky or extremely well-connected. For most ordinary mortals already embarked on a career, our experience to date will influence the direction of our job search; what you have done before, or are doing now, will help to determine what you do next.

However, regardless of whether you want to try and change direction or land the ideal job for the next stage in your chosen career path, being well-prepared is one of the most effective ways that you can enhance your chances of success.

The value of research

'I've sent 200 letters in three months and not had an offer of anything.' So speaks a frustrated job-hunter. He feels he's been trying as hard as he can to find an opening, but all his effort is in vain. Clearly he has been putting in effort, but his problem is too little focus.

Kickstart Tip

It is better to send 20 targeted letters than 200 random ones. This is where putting in the effort to research markets, job opportunities and potential employers thoroughly can really pay dividends.

Effective research holds the key to success – at every stage of the job-hunting process. It encourages a more focused job search, avoiding a scatter-gun approach where applications and inquiries are sent off at random.

Thorough research helps to:

- identify promising market sectors;
- home in on potential job opportunities;
- tailor the initial approach to a target employer;
- increase the relevance of CVs; and
- improve interview performance.

Identifying promising market sectors

The nature of economic life means that some sectors will be booming while others are in decline. Identifying industries in a growth phase is more likely to bring positive results.

You can get a sense of those doing well by skimming through the business pages, or looking at which types of companies are highly valued in the stock market and maintaining those values over the long term. If the shares of companies in any particular sector grouping are generally rising, that's a good sign that analysts and investors think there are healthy growth prospects ahead.

Of course, what does well now could slump in future. The burst in the dot.com bubble during the year 2000 was a useful reminder that sectors that appear golden in the eyes of City investors can quickly be dumped if confidence slips. Nevertheless, it is still a valuable exercise to try to identify where future prospects are likely to be rosy.

Medium- and long-term demographic trends can also be taken into account. The UK's ageing population, for example, suggests that the 'grey pound' will have increasing importance. Services tailored to older age groups should find a gradually expanding customer base.

Homing in on potential job opportunities

If there is a particular sector that appeals, you can then look at it in more depth to identify exactly where the best opportunities lie. Say you are drawn by the IT industry. Under the IT umbrella there are a whole range of different subsectors – software development, hardware supply, web design, consultancy, managing outsourced services and so on.

Your target area may be determined by your skills. If you are a programmer and happy to continue in that line, then clearly your job search will focus largely on the software developers. But if you are a marketing professional, you have more choice. Is one part of the IT industry doing better than the others? Are some companies growing fast, acquiring other businesses and more likely to be in need of new recruits? These are the employers with prospects and therefore of most potential interest to you.

Tailoring the initial approach to a target employer

By researching your chosen sector or specialism, you should come up with a number of names of promising employers. Your research may also indicate a particular hook on which you can hang your initial approach, a topic we look at in detail in Chapter 12, Speculative Approaches.

If you are responding to an advertised vacancy, researching your target company effectively can throw up some nugget of information you can use in your covering letter – perhaps a reference to a recent acquisition, contract deal or new product launch.

Increasing the relevance of CVs

Your CV needs to grab the attention of an individual recruiter in a specific organization. The more you understand about the organization, the better you can tailor your CV to catch the recruiter's eye.

> **Kickstart Tip**
>
> Say you know that your target company is shortly to embark on a two-stage reorganization, as announced at its recent annual general meeting. This is perfect timing because you have just helped to implement such a reorganization at your current company. This should be flagged clearly in your CV.

Perhaps you are trying to switch sectors, but you believe your skills are transferable. You are a legal expert and want to move from a firm of solicitors to a role as a corporate lawyer inside a consultancy. You see that your target employer has recently acquired a French subsidiary. Your CV should not only stress the fact that you have a French degree, but also highlight your ability to speak fluently on commercial topics.

Improving interview performance

Once you reach the interview stage, all your past research can really give you a headstart over other applicants. If you know your subject (in this case the employer, the industry and your own skills) then you should feel less nervous about entering the interview room. Interviewers are always impressed by a candidate who has obviously put effort into finding out about the employer and its marketplace. You are also less likely to be caught off guard by a question referring to some major event about which you know nothing.

Tapping all resources

There are plenty of sources of information available to the innovative job-hunter, whether you are seeking leads on market sectors, career roles or individual employers.
Useful information sources include:

- **National newspapers**
  These are invaluable for high-level reviews of sector dynamics (what's going up, what's in decline) and for giving an idea of some of the more high-profile employers.

- **Regional papers**
  These can be good sources of information on which employers are expanding in the area.

- **Television and radio news**
  As with the press, major companies' expansion or redundancy plans will generally feature on the news.

- **Professional journals and trade press**
  Many industries and professions have their own trade press, offering rich sources of data news on market events.

- **Internet-based newswires**
  Industries and professions are increasingly served by Internet-based news services offering regular bulletins on developments in the sector.

- **Industry, trade and professional bodies**
  These may have information on member firms. Some may have their own internal careers advisers who can offer suggestions as to where potential vacancies may lie.

- **Local business organizations**
  Chambers of commerce and other local, government-supported bodies may have information on local businesses that are expanding.

- **Conference information**
  Many industries or professions run regular conferences where current topical issues are discussed. You don't need to attend to get an idea of what's hot and what's not. Magazines often contain flyers advertising the events.

- **Job fairs**
  These can be useful for those seeking junior management positions, who want to meet a large number of employers currently looking for new employees.

- **Your personal network**
  Insider information – whether rumours of expansion or downsizing, staff shortages or staff redundancies – can help you to contact the right employers at the right time.

Internet-based resources

Most of the sources of information shown above are long-standing and familiar to most job-hunters. However, the modern job-seeker has a great advantage over people who were looking for work just ten years ago: the expansion of the Internet means there is an almost overwhelming amount of data available on virtually every conceivable topic.

If you have access to the Internet at home, this will give you a particularly strong advantage, allowing you the time to search at length for information on potential employers.

Internet-based resources include:

- **Online newswires and newspapers**
  Online newswires, often devoted to a particular industry or sector, report recent events involving key organizations. In addition, traditional national newspapers increasingly reproduce their hard-copy articles on their websites. Some also have useful search facilities. You could try looking at:

www.ft.com	*Financial Times*
www.guardian.co.uk	*Guardian*
www.telegraph.co.uk	*Daily Telegraph*
www.thetimes.co.uk	*The Times*

- **Company websites**
  Even medium-sized or small companies frequently now have their own websites. The

extent of the information they provide varies hugely. Some may simply show their address and contact details. Others will include extensive information on their products and services, their annual reports and accounts, their corporate outlook and press releases going back several years. There may also be biographical information on key directors and examples of recent press coverage. Best of all, details of current vacancies may even be given online.

- **Online jobsites**
  These not only provide you with vacancies to consider applying for, but also give an indication of the sectors where there may be most current recruitment activity. We look at these again in Chapter 8, Advertised Openings.

- **Other general or professional websites**
  Professional associations or representative bodies, such as the Recruitment and Employment Confederation (REC), will have contact links to websites of member firms. We include the REC web address in the Appendix. Other company directory sites such as www.scoot.com may be useful for conducting general searches.

Researching likely employers

As you start to identify potentially promising employers, there are a number of things to look out for. These include:

- **Recent financial performance**
  Is the organization in a growth phase or are profits in danger of slipping into decline?

- **Recent commercial events**
  Has the company been acquiring rivals? Have new products been launched?

- **Other organizational developments**
  Has the group restructured, relocated or shaken up its management team? Look out for any links between you and the management. For example, did the new finance director train with your old accountancy firm?

- **Geographical spread**
  Is there a regional focus that could benefit you? Does the organization have overseas connections you might be able to turn to your advantage?

- **IT issues**

  Has the employer recently announced its intention to switch to a new IT system with which you have extensive experience?

- **Corporate culture**

  How does the organization perceive itself? Is it a young gun, a maverick or a long-standing member of the corporate establishment? How do industry commentators see it? Does the culture fit well with your own personality?

- **Bad press**

  Has the organization been criticized for poor employment practices or for the declining quality of its products and services?

This kind of information can help steer you away from organizations with poor employment prospects, and towards those with potential need for your services. This not only helps to stop you wasting your time following up dud ideas, but gives you potential hooks on which to make speculative approaches.

The importance of SMEs for job-hunters

Most of us know the names of the major employers. We see their names in the press, on the television and on the packages of the products we buy. It is natural that many job-hunters limit their search to these names that they know. They shouldn't.

Firing off a letter to the chairman, chief executive or personnel director of a FTSE 100 company is likely to prove a waste of time and effort. If there is no obvious reason why this company or this director should be interested in you, your letter will receive hardly a glance. The problem is that because these major organizations are the most visible and therefore they attract the most direct applications.

However, canny job-hunters recognize the wealth of job opportunities that lie beyond the corporate giants – within small and medium-sized enterprises (SMEs). According to Department of Trade and Industry statistics, SMEs employ around 55 per cent of the UK's employees. There are around 3.7 million active UK businesses, of which 99.2 per cent are classed as small (employing fewer than 50 employees), 0.8 per cent are medium-sized (employing between 50 and 249 employees) and just 0.2 per cent – equivalent to around 7,000 businesses – are large (employing 500 or more people).

> ## Kickstart Tip
>
> Given that dynamic SMEs go through significant growth phases, small and medium-sized businesses also create many new jobs; in fact, they create the majority of the new jobs in the employment market. They aren't just looking to replace leavers, but to staff up as they increase the extent of their operations.

For SMEs, finding quality managers and staff can appear as daunting as finding a quality employer can for the individual job-hunter. If you clearly have skills, experience or sector knowledge of direct relevance, then a small or mid-sized firm may well be over-joyed to hear from you.

In particular, SMEs with ambition, that want to grow rapidly, can also provide excellent promotion prospects and new challenges for their staff. Once inside the organization, you may find the personal satisfaction of being a bigger fish in a smaller pond outweighs any initial concerns about not working for a nationally known name. Many people often prefer the working environment of the SME, which often gives a greater sense of involvement.

Chapter summary: key points

- Effective and thorough research is a vital element for any successful job hunt.
- Use the information you find to sharpen the focus of your job search: 20 targeted applications are far better than 200 untargeted ones.
- Home in on promising employers in thriving market sectors.
- Information on specific organizations can give you the opening to make an initial approach about suitable vacancies.
- The more you know about a potential employer, the more effectively you can tailor your CV.
- The more thorough your research, the better your interview performance is likely to be.
- Tap all available resources for information, including the press (national, regional and trade), broadcast news, Internet-based newswires, industry, trade and professional bodies, local business organizations, conference information and your own personal contacts.

- The Internet is an extremely useful tool for the job-hunter. Make use of online news sources, company websites and jobsites for seeking out likely job opportunities.
- Look out for any news on financial performance and commercial, organizational, IT and cultural developments, both positive and negative.
- Don't just focus on the major employers; SMEs can provide stimulating opportunities as they grow and develop.

Chapter <u>6</u>

Preparing Your Marketing Material

f the job-hunting process is equivalent to a sales campaign, then the curriculum vitae represents its key marketing material. The CV encapsulates the particular skills and attributes you possess that you hope will catch the employer's eye.

The aim of the CV

Be clear on the role the CV plays in your job search. Its function is *not* to get you a job *offer*; its function *is* to get you a job *interview*.

Think of the CV as an hors d'oeuvre that will whet the recruiter's appetite and create a hunger to meet you. You want to give a flavour of your strengths, your achievements and the ways you have contributed to the success of past employers. You want to create curiosity in the recruiter's mind about how your skills could be put to their advantage.

Understanding this true goal should help you prepare a CV that catches the recruiter's eye. You don't need to include your entire life history. Your aim is to offer a succinct summary of key career achievements to date, supplemented by basic factual data such as your educational qualifications and contact details.

Kickstart Tip

When drafting your CV, try to think of it not just from your own personal perspective, but also from that of the recruiting reader. Imagine the poor person responsible for ploughing through a pile of 100 CVs and trying to select a shortlist for interview. Then think about how you can make that person's life easier. If you help this person, you also help your chances of your CV being put in the interview pile rather than jettisoned into the waste paper bin.

By the way, helping the CV sifter spot your potential and preparing an eye-catching CV does not mean using fluorescent pink paper. That might stop your CV getting lost in the in-tray, but such a florid approach is unlikely to impress.

We will look in detail at the kind of CV you want to produce, but first, a word on the kind of CV you should avoid.

Classic CV errors

Common errors include:

- CVs that are too long (over three pages);
- CVs that are too short (one page);
- lack of sensible structure;
- failure to link the CV's contents – your skills and experience – to the job sought;
- inclusion of irrelevant data;
- uninformative lists of roles or responsibilities;
- unexplained gaps in work experience; and
- spelling and grammatical errors.

Many of these mistakes can be traced back to laziness in the process of preparing the CV. For example, some people think they can just maintain a 'rolling CV' where their latest job is simply tacked onto the bottom of what has gone before. At the top may be that position you had as a production assistant's assistant for six months in 1985, where you spent most of your time making cups of tea for other people. At the bottom sits your current job as head of current affairs, which the recruiter may or may not notice, depending whether they can be bothered to read through that far. This CV has become merely a list of jobs, which may or may not be relevant to the role applied for.

The 'rolling CV' approach is likely to end up with a CV that commits the classic mistakes of being too lengthy, poorly structured and irrelevant. While the information contained in the rolling list may be useful as a memory jogger, it should remain for your eyes only and never be sent out to an employer.

Tips for a top CV

Drawing up a CV that will fulfil its aim – generating an invitation for you to come for an interview – takes a little time and effort. To make sure that effort isn't wasted, try to apply the following guidelines for content and structure.

The perfect length

Our research found strong preference for the ideal CV being just two pages long; 70 per cent of our recruiters said this was the ideal. Therefore, most people should aim to include all relevant information in just two pages; the CV is not the life story you have always wanted to write. The example of a CV we have included in Figure 6.1 fits on two pages of A4.

That said, a three-page CV was preferred by almost a quarter of our sample recruiters. If you are a senior executive with 25 years' worth of career achievements to summarize, you may need that third page to convey your value sufficiently. However, a CV should *never* be more than three pages long.

You don't need to challenge yourself to produce a CV shorter than two pages. To fit enough information into one page would probably require such a small typeface that your recruiter would have severe eyestrain by the end of it.

Adapting your CV: making content relevant

Ideally, every key element of your CV should be relevant to the job you are applying for, to the employer or to the industry sector. Bear this in mind when deciding which of your skills to highlight and how to describe them. Free yourself from the tyranny of using the same CV for every application.

This means you should tweak your CV every time you respond to an advertised job vacancy or send your CV with a speculative letter to a targeted employer. You cannot simply roll out the same CV each time; the content must be adjusted to reflect the particular skills requested in the advert, or the specific circumstances that make you think an employer will be interested in talking to you.

By the way, information about your family is not relevant to any job application. Experience suggests that men are more often guilty of this particular CV offence than women. There is nothing wrong with being proud of your family and their achievements, but a CV does not need to tell the recruiter where your children are attending university. Information about husbands, wives, children and pets should be reserved for small talk – not included in your prime marketing document.

Dating your career progress

Dates should be included for all the past jobs you have held, including the start and end date in terms of month and year. Stating these dates in years only is too broad and could make an employer wonder whether you are trying to obscure some gaps in employment. Recruiters will be on the lookout for any such gaps so try to give a complete picture. If you spent a year travelling, say so.

While no recruiter would advocate lying on a CV, if you tried a job for three months, realized it was a mistake and quickly moved on to something else, it might be simpler to leave it out. This is particularly true if the experience occurred some years ago and is irrelevant for your current job application.

Health issues

Remember that the employer is trying to recruit the best person for the job. The general rule applies that you should try to avoid including anything that might conflict with that picture. People who have spent some time out of work due to health problems should particularly bear this in mind. Mental illness is included here. You may have recovered fully and even be a stronger, more supportive, team-focused individual as a result of the experience, but getting this message across in a CV is extremely difficult.

The employer's predetermined picture of 'the best person for the job' probably does not include someone with a history of mental illness, back problems or other health complaints that might cause them to take extended periods off work.

Of course, if you are asked at a later date to state whether you have any such health concerns, you should never lie about them. It's just that such information is always best revealed only after you have got a foot in the employer's door, met the interviewer face to face, impressed with your clear ability and had a chance to start building rapport and a relationship.

Other content to avoid

Potentially contentious areas such as politics and religion should also be avoided. Remember you are trying to appeal to someone whose personal philosophy and outlook you know nothing about. You don't want to do anything that could possibly alienate them before they have a chance to meet you.

Another word of warning: never include reasons for leaving a past job on the CV. You might feel that your boss was an unbearable tyrant and your row was perfectly understandable, but the CV reader could interpret this to mean you are difficult to work with and have a problem with authority. Let the recruiter ask you about your reasons for moving on at the interview if he is interested. Explaining your actions in person is far easier than doing so in one line on a CV.

Nor should you waste space stating your career objectives. The employer will assume that the fact you have applied for the job means that it meets your current career aims. The employer is more interested in how you can help the organization meet its objectives, rather than the other way around.

Salary information should also be avoided. The aim of your CV is to hook the employer's initial interest, which you then develop at the interview stage. Salary discussions come way down the line, at a stage when the employer is keen to get you on board. If there is scope for talking your salary package up, you certainly don't want to have given away upfront in your CV how much you would accept. Keep these financial cards close to your chest and play them only when appropriate.

Personal taste

Not everyone agrees on the ideal CV content. In our research we asked survey respondents to rate the importance to them of various items. Overall, they indicated that the most important element in a CV is a list of the applicant's achievements. The reason for this is clear – it helps to make the recruiter's job significantly easier.

Kickstart Tip

By flagging up what you see as your achievements, the recruiter can more easily take a view on whether those are relevant to the job on offer. This is therefore an absolutely essential element of any CV.

After that the most important elements overall were considered to be the candidate's age or date of birth, reasons for leaving the last job, salary information, additional training and a personal summary statement. Of least importance to our survey respondents were references, hobbies and interests and family details.

You may notice that some of these 'important' elements appear to contradict the advice given earlier in this chapter. This is largely down to differences in perspective between applicants and recruiters. Items that recruiters see as most important are those that can help them filter applicants *out* of the running, as well as into the interview pile. Items most important for applicants are simply those that keep them in the running.

As a job applicant, it may well be in your best interests to leave out certain information recruiters say is important. As noted in Chapter 2, Understanding the Employer, although recruiters will want to know your reasons for leaving your last job, your explanation is probably best left until the interview, particularly if you feel you can do this adequately only in person. You might also feel it in your interests to omit your salary details from your own CV.

As for including a personal summary statement, over 25 per cent of our respondents did not see this as important. Such summary statements can be a waste of space and are sometimes used by job applicants who have taken the concept of the CV as a marketing document too literally. Introducing your CV with a sentence such as 'Highly commercial, computer-literate financial professional seeks dynamic management opportunity' wastes your time and the reader's. It is better to let your CV show the employer you have these skills and this drive by means of the experience you describe.

Woolly words

Be sharp when writing your CV. Certain words and phrases, which obscure real meaning, are red flags to an experienced recruiter; if you are called for an interview, they may well be queried then.

Examples of such woolly words to avoid include:

- 'involved in', as in 'I was involved in the implementation of a new accounts software package'. Does this mean you actually helped to choose the package and install the new software, or were sent on a training course to learn how to use it once it was introduced?
- 'assisted with', as in 'I assisted with the induction of new staff'. Does that mean you helped to run a training course on office procedures, or you simply showed new employees to their desks on day one?
- 'knowledge of', as in 'I gained knowledge of new promotional techniques'. Does that mean you researched and assessed new marketing campaigns for recommendation to the board, or just read an article during your commute to work?

There are many variations of the above, including 'exposed to', 'participated in' and so on. Make sure you can justify the use of such statements in a way that shows you have real skills that could be valuable to a new employer. Even better, state what your involvement, assistance or knowledge was in plain English on the CV in the first place. Try to use active or dynamic words rather than passive ones.

Layout and structure

There are two key types of CV: the historical and the functional.

Historical CVs

The historical CV, which is the most common form, takes the reader through your career job by job. Although you could do this in chronological order, future employers are most interested in what you have been doing most recently. Our research found an overwhelming preference for jobs being shown in order of the most recent first (preferred by 94 per cent of survey respondents).

Job titles can mean many different things in different organizations, so you should explain exactly what your responsibilities were. Include an explanation of the individual you reported to within the organization, and who reported to you.

Functional CVs

Functional CVs, as the name suggests, emphasize the nature of the work you have done, rather than the chronological structure of your career history. Functional CVs group the applicant's experience under headings such as Production, Sales, Management, Finance or Recruitment. They then give a brief explanation of your experience in these areas.

Names of actual employers, positions held and dates come at the bottom of the functional CV, accompanied by no explanatory information. The functional CV format can therefore be appealing to people who have jumped frequently between jobs and who want to try and divert attention away from this fact by highlighting their functional experience.

Despite the attraction of this format for the job-hunter, our research clearly shows that recruiters overwhelmingly prefer to receive historical, reverse chronological order,

Personal Details	**MARK PRICE**
	Date of Birth: 30 September 1969
Contact Details	57 Defoe Road, Kingston, Surrey
	Tel: 020 8887 7605
	E-mail: m.price@aolinternet.co.uk
Education	Kingsbury High School
	7 O Levels
	3 A Levels: Maths, Economics, Geography
	London School of Economics
	B.Sc (Econ) – 2:1 degree
Professional Qualifications	Associate of the Chartered Institute of Management Accountants 1995 – first time passes
Computer Experience	Excel, Word, Wordpro, Sun Accounts, Peoplesoft

POSITION HISTORY

Aug 1996 – Present	**NEXUS GLOBAL**
	Nexus is a FTSE 100 company with a global turnover in excess of £2bn and over 50,000 employees worldwide. Primary business activities are contract logistics and international freight forwarding.
April 1998 – Present	*FINANCIAL PLANNING MANAGER*

- Development of a fully integrated management information reporting system, establishing a consistent approach to business performance analysis, reporting and management review;
- Production and distribution of all Group reports and preparation of monthly Chairman's business commentary for presentation of results;
- Co-ordination of the three-year Corporate Plan process, financially evaluating corporate strategy and communicating the annual budget targets to the businesses;
- Management of the quarterly forecasting process.

Achievements:
- Spearheaded the restructuring of the department, recruiting a new team and repositioning its role with a clear focus on the commercial issues, such as:
  - Development of reporting by division and market segment;
  - New procedures governing negotiation of supplier contracts;
  - Evaluation of promotional activity.

Aug 1996 – April 1998   *FINANCIAL CONTROLLER*
Of operating subsidiary with turnover of £225m and operating profit £37m

- Set up financial planning and analysis, systems and stock control, including the recruitment of 33 new staff. Established policy, procedures and functional structures to support a multi-site operation;
- Co-ordinated the budget and forecast processes and determination of commercial priorities and financial targets by business stream;

Figure 6.1 A sample historical CV

- Management of the capital investment programme and financial evaluation of opportunities.

Achievements:
- Recruited and established the FP&A function comprising 33 staff in finance, systems and stock control;
- Delivered divisional profit objectives in each of three consecutive years, achieved through: carefully targeted sales activity, strong cost control and focus on investment returns.

Oct 1991 – Aug 1996	**FRENCH KLIEN INTERNATIONAL** Clinical research organization in the pharmaceutical industry ($500m turnover worldwide)

Sept 1994 – Aug 1996   ***BUSINESS PROCESSES CONSULTANT***
- Formed and led a business process re-engineering team to enable the finance department to analyse, assess and re-engineer their business processes and systems;
- Developed excellence within the finance processes to meet or exceed customers' requirements and expectations;
- Identified unsatisfactory or obsolete business practices and developed solutions to meet company's business needs.

Achievements:
- Reduced the time taken to produce the month-end accounts pack from 12 to 6 days;
- Identified, analysed and evaluated significant project, financial or associated business risks;
- Improved existing working practices and standards.

Oct 1991 – Sept 1994   ***SYSTEMS ACCOUNTANT***
- Developed and improved financial business systems in partnership with users;
- Provided application training courses and documentation for systems administrators and end-users at all levels.

Achievements:
- The successful worldwide roll-out of information management systems;
- Project-managed the introduction and implementation of systems into newly acquired companies.

Aug 1990 – Oct 1991   **NETWORK TELECOM**
Primary business activities are semiconductor manufacture and telecommunications with turnover of £30 million.

FINANCIAL ANALYST
- Analysed product sales, mixes and margins;
- Financial reporting and performance evaluation;
- Advised areas of poor performance.

Personal Interests   Football, skiing, scuba-diving, travel, amateur dramatics and jazz.

CVs. You should therefore try to use the historical format, instead of the functional approach, if at all possible.

General layout

Try not to cram every centimetre of each page with words. Presentation is important for creating an immediately positive impression; white space helps the reader to take in the information you provide. You can also make use of bold type for headings and bullet points for summarizing key data.

Photos

You don't normally need to worry about including a photo, unless this is specifically requested. The majority of our survey respondents had no preference about whether applicants attached mugshots to their CVs or not and 34 per cent specifically said they preferred not to see such photos. Let the recruiter find out what you look like when you turn up at the interview.

Analysing your own CV – the litmus test

When you have completed a first draft of your CV, put it aside and walk away. Do something else for half an hour and then review your efforts. This is a useful process because it's amazing how much more easily you can spot errors such as spelling mistakes, typos and unclear statements when you haven't already been staring at them for three hours.

Apart from checking for these basic mistakes, you should review the draft CV to see whether it meets its key aims of indicating how you and your skills could add value to the target employer. Try to be dispassionate and ask yourself honestly whether the CV you have written:

- highlights your achievements;
- indicates the relevance of your experience;
- conveys the breadth of your experience; and
- shows the depth of your experience, including all relevant specialist skills and knowledge.

The litmus test is: would you want to give yourself an interview based on the CV in front of you? If you have any doubts about the content in any areas, rewrite them. This time spent upfront, before you have had any contact at all with the target employer, could determine your ultimate job-hunting success.

Once you are happy with the CV, it may still be worth getting a second opinion from a trusted friend or relation. You may believe that a certain acronym is widely understood, but you could be wrong. If your trusted friend suggests some alterations, consider them carefully. If you agree, adjust the CV, but you don't have to accept all advice you receive. The CV is your document, your marketing material, and it must be true to you.

How to handle application forms

When you respond to some advertised job vacancies you may be required to complete an application form. As we explained in Chapter 3, Planning an Effective Job Search, this is particularly likely for public sector jobs.

Unfortunately, application forms aren't always easy to fill out. They generally require extensive details of your experience and explanations of why you believe yourself to be suitable.

When you know you have a ready-made CV to hand, it can be tempting either to ignore the form altogether, or to fill in many of its boxes with the terse phrase 'See CV'. This is in fact what many people do.

Do not be tempted to do this yourself!

The recruiting organization hasn't sent you the form just so you can refer it back to your CV. The form is intended to generate comparable information from candidates to improve the likelihood that the most suitable will be called for interview.

If you want a chance of an interview invite, you *must* fill in the form and you must do so completely. You just have to apply the same techniques you would use in adapting your CV to a specific job vacancy.

Apply the following approach to show yourself at your best in the application form:

- **Take or make several copies of the blank form so you can practise filling it in**
  If you dive straight in you can easily misjudge the space available for particular answers. For example, you could have decided there are three key attributes that

make you highly suitable for the role, but you have only highlighted one and a half before you run out of space. While you can usually attach extra sheets of paper with relevant information, the less you need to do this, the more professional your form will appear.

- **Answer all questions**
  Application forms give you less control over content than your own CV. If the form asks for your age and any health problems, you do have to give answers. If you are called for an interview and your form contains gaps, these will certainly be queried.

- **Apply the same rules as for drafting a CV**
  This means you should be concise, use clear English and tailor each answer to fit the job for which you are applying. Sell yourself! Highlight the key skills and expertise you have to offer that will add most value to the employer.

- **Take a photocopy of the form before you send it off**
  If you are invited for an interview you will need this copy to remind yourself what you said. Otherwise you could be caught out if the interviewer comments on your explanation of how managing a custard-making factory had given you the skills you need for managing an old people's home. What particular aspects were you highlighting?

Letters that open doors

A good covering letter is rated as being important by over half the recruiters in our survey. In fact, the covering letter is one of the most underutilized tools in the job-hunting game.

Kickstart Tip

If you put a little effort into making your covering letter stand out, you can gain a valuable advantage over the competition, one that may get you the interview you want. The covering letter usually provides the first contact you have with the recruiter, before your CV even receives a glance. It therefore creates the first impression of the kind of person you are.

Most covering letters simply say, 'Please find enclosed my CV in relation to your recent advertisement in the *Financial Times . . .*' and *nothing more.* This is unoriginal, uninformative and uninspiring and adds no extra value to your application.

Clever content

We asked our survey respondents what they considered to be essential information for inclusion in the covering letter. Over 80 per cent said the letter must contain the reasons for the application, while almost two-thirds also believed that stating the relevance of the applicant's experience was also on the 'must have' list.

Including a brief career history in your covering letter is not necessary. Less than a quarter of our survey respondents said this was essential.

What you want to do is to make yourself and your application stand out immediately from the growing pile of applications on the recruiter's desk. The way to do this is to pick out a couple of points that will highlight your suitability, which you can flag up in the covering letter. Try to pick characteristics stressed in the job ad and explicitly state why you believe you have them.

Kickstart Tip

Perhaps you feel that your recent multi-site experience in a brewery, which involved introducing a new management information system into each location, is one of your strong selling points. If so, mention it in the covering letter. Don't just say you have the skills advertised; demonstrate why or how it is that you have them.

Apart from that, don't forget a few basics. Specify exactly what job you are applying for, and where and when the advertisement you saw appeared. A recruitment consultancy receives a large number of responses to a large number of job advertisements. If you don't say exactly what you are applying for, they may not necessarily take the trouble to try to work it out.

Type your letter, rather than send in a handwritten one, unless this is specifically requested (for handwriting analysis). Most people's handwriting isn't exactly textbook style and you want to make your letter as easy to read as possible. This means you can

Mr Brendan Wood
GKW Executive Selection
16 Hamilton Street
St James's
London W1

Dear Sir

Re: Position of Finance Director – Business Services Ref: D141 – *Financial Times* **19/4/2001**

Please find enclosed a copy of my CV in response to the above advertisement.

You will see from my CV that I am currently Finance Director of a rapidly expanding business services organization. Having restructured the finance function, implemented new accounting systems and improved the quality of management information, I am now seeking a more commercial role similar to that advertised.

I believe that I can offer directly relevant experience in a number of key areas.

1. **Staff Management** – currently responsible for a total of 32 staff, I directly supervise four departmental heads. I have increased the quality of staff in line with a planned decrease in staff numbers. Morale and motivation has improved considerably with the successful development of a strong customer service mentality.

2. **Systems Development** – directly responsible for the specification and successful implementation of new payroll and management accounting systems. These projects were completed within budget and ahead of schedule. There have been considerable efficiency gains while the quality and quantity of management information has increased.

3. **Improved Profitability** – made significant contribution to the company's profits through prudent management of costs, education of sales managers, effective cash management and proactive tax planning.

I am extremely interested in the advertised position and believe I can make a significant contribution to your client's business. I would welcome the opportunity of an interview to demonstrate the direct relevance of my experience to your client.

Yours sincerely

Peter Povey

Peter Povey

Figure 6.2 A sample covering letter

also make effective use of underlining or bold text if that helps highlight the qualities you have to offer.

Finally, don't let your covering letter run away with itself. Two-thirds of our survey respondents said the ideal length was between one and two pages. One in five preferred them to be less than a page long.

Sending off your CV

Snail mail has now been surpassed by email as the preferred method of delivering a CV. Our research found that almost half of the recruiters and line managers in our survey said they preferred to receive CVs by email, with just 21 per cent still opting for hard copies received in the post. Only 8 per cent like faxes.

The best approach for sending in your CV, therefore, unless you are told otherwise, is to email it as a Word document attached to an explanatory email message – the online equivalent of the covering letter. Although you could send your covering letter as an attachment as well, the email message is a better approach.

Just as with a traditional covering letter, you want your covering email to catch the application sifter's eye. So the same principles about content apply to the email as to the letter – pick out some key skills you possess, that you consider most appropriate to the employer or the role you seek, and illustrate how you have put them to use recently.

Similarly, maintain the same level of formality in the covering email as you would in the covering letter. Although email grammar and style tend to be far more relaxed than that used in formal letter writing, don't forget that you are using the email in a very formal situation – to present yourself to a potential new employer. You should therefore avoid using any trendy email shorthand.

Think about how much writing you can fit on a PC screen and make your email that length. You want to make reading the email simple for recruiters, so avoid being too wordy and making them scroll down through several screens.

Chapter summary: key points

- The CV provides the main marketing material in your job-hunting campaign.
- The CV's aim is to gain you an interview, not the job itself.
- Tailor the contents as closely as possible to the requirements of the target job.
- Most people are best served by drafting a historical CV describing jobs held in reverse chronological order.
- Don't write a CV longer than three pages. Most people just need two.
- Avoid anything that can make the recruiter suspicious, such as unexplained gaps in your career history.
- Avoid potentially controversial content such as political affiliations.
- Allow time to review and improve your draft CV before sending it off; ask a friend to look at it, as well as your covering letter.
- If you are asked to complete an application form, make sure you do so fully.
- Practise answering the questions on a photocopy of the original form.
- Answer all questions.
- Write a covering letter that makes you stand out by highlighting three or four key attributes that make you the best person for the job.
- Sending CVs by email is increasingly common. If you do so, write a covering email that follows the same approach as a covering letter.

Chapter 7

Tips from the Top

Motivation and positive thinking play an important part in helping to achieve career goals. The individuals in your chosen career who impress and inspire you can teach you something about what it takes to be a success.

In researching this book we asked some noted celebrities and recognized leaders in their field three questions:

- What was the best career advice they ever received?
- What key career advice would they give to other people?
- What personal characteristics do they look for in others?

We hope their replies will give you fresh inspiration if your job search is flagging or you need an extra motivational boost to kickstart your career.

Lord Sheppard of Didgemere

Lord Sheppard of Didgemere is one of Britain's most respected business leaders. Born Allen Sheppard, he qualified as an accountant and worked for almost 20 years in the motor industry. He then moved to Grand Metropolitan and, as Chairman and Chief Executive between 1986 and 1996, he refocused the company into an international, world-leading food and drink business. He was given a seat in the House of Lords in 1994.

Best career advice
'I know you have enjoyed your 20 years in the motor industry and you have gone much further than you ever thought you would. However, what happens in the next 20 years? Isn't it time to move on?'

This resulted in me joining GrandMet to run Watneys.

What single piece of career advice would you give?
Never 'leave' a job. Concentrate on why the new opportunity is right for you. In other words, think positively.

What personal characteristics do you look for in others?
Courage (i.e. sensible risk-taking) and vision (practical strategic thinking).

Michael Grade

Michael Grade spent around a quarter of a century at the top of television, working for London Weekend Television and the BBC before becoming Head of Channel 4. He brought the UK the likes of *ER*, *Friends*, *Cheers* and the live transmission of Live Aid, and financed highly successful films such as *Four Weddings and a Funeral* and *Trainspotting*. He left Channel 4 to head up First Leisure, the bars and bowling group, and has subsequently taken over Pinewood Studios and launched a venture capital fund investing in the leisure and media sectors.

Best career advice
Stick to what you know – and know what you don't know.

What single piece of career advice would you give?
Always research the prospective employer. Sample their products, advertising and image. Make a constructive analysis that shows you have thought carefully about the company.

What personal characteristics do you look for in others?
Someone who has thought through any opinions they offer and who is not easily moved from their position, but is willing to listen to contrary opinions.

Lord MacLaurin

Lord MacLaurin was Managing Director and Chairman of Tesco for 18 years, playing a major role in turning the food retailer's performance around and making it the UK leader in its sector. He has held many other senior appointments, including serving on the board of Whitbread and Vodafone. He also has a passion for cricket and is Chairman of the England and Wales Cricket Board.

Best career advice
Know the business inside out – from top to bottom. Try to understand what everybody contributes to the organization.

What single piece of career advice would you give?
Find a job which really excites you – then give it all you have.

What personal characteristics do you look for in others?
I will always look for a rounded person who has wide interests. I am always keen on people who have played team games, which helps very much in business.

Sir Terence Conran

Sir Terence Conran, who founded Habitat in 1964, has made himself an international reputation as a designer, retailer and restaurateur. He became closely involved in retailing through Storehouse, from which he retired in 1990. Conran's stable of successful London restaurants have also become well-known names, not least Bibendum, situated in the art deco former headquarters of Michelin.

Best career advice
I've never had any, because I've never had a career.

What single piece of career advice would you give?
Be sure that you will be happy in your job.

What personal characteristics do you look for in others?
Honesty, energy, ambition, hard work and dedication.

Nicola Horlick

Nicola Horlick is a successful City fund manager. A symbol of high-flying female success, she became a public face when her bank suspended her, on suspicion that she was about to defect with her team to a rival bank. Horlick responded by flying to the bank's head office in Frankfurt and challenging her employers in the full media glare. She has since launched a new fund for Société Général: SG Asset Management. A mother of six, she lost her eldest daughter to leukaemia.

Best career advice
If you keep your head down and work hard, someone will notice and that is the way to the top. Politics isn't!

What single piece of career advice would you give?
Choose your boss carefully – in a large organization you must have someone with power as a sponsor.

What personal characteristics do you look for in others?
I want people who are articulate, thorough and decisive. This last factor is essential for a fund manager. A stock is either a buy or a sell – I don't want people who sit on the fence.

Michael Parkinson

Michael Parkinson is a highly acclaimed writer, broadcaster and television interviewer – one of the most respected UK chat show hosts. He began his career, after National Service, working as a local and national newspaper journalist, before moving on to television current affairs. In 1998, after an extended absence, he made a triumphant return to the BBC.

Best career advice
Keep moving. Explore the limits of what you have to offer.

What single piece of career advice would you give?
Never fear.

What personal characteristics do you look for in others?
Optimism, fearlessness and humour.

Raymond Blanc

Raymond Blanc came to England in 1972 and has become a culinary superstar, setting up the acclaimed restaurant and country house hotel, Le Manoir aux Quat'Saisons in Oxfordshire. Blanc has trained many young Michelin-starred chefs and is also a successful writer and broadcaster.

Best career advice

Do not give away trust; it is far too important a commodity. When you do, once your trust is deserved, credit people's intelligence; you will receive much in return.

What single piece of career advice would you give?

Talent is not enough to give you success. You will need an iron willpower to carry you through the challenges you will inevitably face.

What personal characteristics do you look for in others?

- Intelligence (emotional and intellectual), sensitivity, creativity, imagination.
- The ability to listen, to be reflective, to be analytical.
- Ability to reinvent or redefine yourself.
- A person who has the ability to change shape. (I could not contemplate employing a square, round circle or a perfect triangle.)
- A team player with the understanding that the sublimes can only be reached through the performance and achievements of each team member.
- Ability to understand and value what is beautiful.

Sir Chay Blyth, CBE, BEM

Sir Chay Blyth is a former soldier in the Parachute Regiment, but he made his name for rowing the Atlantic and for being the first man to sail around the world against the prevailing winds and currents. He has since made a successful business out of yacht racing, organizing and raising sponsorship for high-profile sailing challenges, including the BT Global Challenge.

Best career advice

When faced with two alternatives, always choose the bolder!

What single piece of career advice would you give?

Research the company and prepare questions. 'Time spent in reconnaissance is time seldom wasted.'

What personal characteristics do you look for in others?

Enthusiasm for the company, self-discipline, self-projection, and the ability to understand and practise visualization.

Jack Charlton, OBE

Jack Charlton played almost 800 games in a 20-year career for Leeds United, winning the Championship, the FA Cup, the League Cup and the European Fairs Cup. In 1967 he was voted footballer of the year. As a manager, he took Sheffield Wednesday and Middlesbrough to promotion, and the Irish national side to two World Cups and a European Championship.

Best career advice

Never tell lies. (You will need a good memory if you do.)

What single piece of career advice would you give?

Look him [the recruiter] in the eyes, listen and nod.

What personal characteristics do you look for in others?

Listening, nodding and paying attention.

Lord Coe, OBE

Sebastian Coe, twice Olympic 1500 metres champion, became a household name in the 1980s for his sporting prowess on the running track. He entered politics after retiring from competitive athletics and acted as Conservative MP for Falmouth and Camborne in Cornwall until 1997, after which he was appointed Private Secretary to the Leader of the Opposition, William Hague.

Best career advice
Brendan Foster [fellow athlete] told me to get an accountant when I started to compete successfully.

What personal characteristics do you look for in others?
Above all, the will to succeed, underpinned by self-motivation.

Harvey Goldsmith

Harvey Goldsmith has spent 30 years at the top of the music promotion business. In 1986 he organized the famous Live Aid concert in support of African famine victims in just 10 weeks, bringing together a record-breaking number of artists on one stage. His other great successes have included staging Pavarotti in the Park, when Italian tenor Luciano Pavarotti sang to thousands in London's Hyde Park.

Best career advice
Never take 'No' for an answer.

What single piece of career advice would you give?
If you believe in a career pathway, look at every angle and perspective until you achieve a result.

What personal characteristics do you look for in others?
- Can they do the job? In other words, are they capable of carrying out the work that they are leading you to believe they can?
- Will they fit in with the rest of the team?
- Their level of enthusiasm.

Barry Hearn

Barry Hearn, a trained chartered accountant, became fully involved in sports promotion when TV was first discovering snooker. Now recognized as a leading sports promoter, and head of the Matchroom organization, he has worked closely with famous sporting names such as Steve Davis and Chris Eubank.

Best career advice
Take the challenge – prepare to make mistakes, but only once!

What single piece of career advice would you give?
Will it be fun?

What personal characteristics do you look for in others?
Dedication, integrity, honesty, openness, capacity to work hard and being prepared to admit mistakes or shortcomings.

Prue Leith

Prue Leith, a South African educated in Paris, began her career as a Cordon Bleu cook in London, establishing a catering business from her bedsit in Earls Court. From these humble beginnings she developed a thriving restaurant and catering business, serving thousands of meals a day in famous venues such as the Queen Elizabeth Conference Centre and the Natural History Museum. She is also an acclaimed writer and journalist.

Best career advice
Stick at it. Starting things is easy – a quarrel, a novel, a baby, weeding the lawn. But maintaining the quarrel, finishing the novel, doing the whole lawn is what sorts out the men from the boys. And babies turn into horrible teenagers before they become lovely again. Doggedness is all.

What single piece of career advice would you give?
Don't work for anyone you don't admire.

What personal characteristics do you look for in others?
I've got to warm to them. Why spend 40 hours a week with someone you don't like?

Ron Dennis

Ron Dennis joined the Brabham Racing Team as a mechanic in the 1960s and from the start showed determination to succeed as an engineer and as a businessman. Now head of McLaren International, one of the most successful racing teams in Formula One, he is hailed as an excellent manager.

Best career advice
My mother, when I first left school, told me that whatever job I undertook in the future, no matter how small or seemingly unimportant the task, I should do it to the absolute best of my ability.

What single piece of career advice would you give?
Always give 100 per cent and take pride in all that you do. Be conscientious, work hard and demonstrate commitment and loyalty. These things will all hold you in good stead.

What personal characteristics do you look for in others?
I look for someone who listens carefully to the questions I ask and gives considered and articulate responses. All too often in interviews, possibly due to nerves, people don't listen properly to what is being said to them and therefore don't always give the appropriate response.

David Lloyd

Born into a tennis-playing family, David Lloyd became a professional tennis player in his teens and subsequently spent 17 years on the professional circuit. After retiring from the sport he ran indoor tennis centres in Canada before setting up the UK's first indoor tennis and fitness centre in Middlesex. The business grew, expanding around the UK, and then successfully floated on the stock market before the clubs were ultimately sold to

Whitbread. David has subsequently set up a new business, Next Generation Clubs, providing health and leisure complexes. He has maintained his involvement with tennis and was captain of the British Davis Cup Team from 1997 to 2000.

Best career advice
Believe in yourself.

What single piece of career advice would you give?
Whatever you do, you must look forward to the day ahead. As soon as you stop enjoying what you do, get out.

What personal characteristics do you look for in others?
Honesty, ambition and team spirit.

Michael Lynagh

Michael Lynagh, a Rugby Union hero, is acclaimed as Australia's greatest-ever fly half. He played 72 times for his country, scoring 911 points. He captained the Australian team for three years before he retired from the international game in 1995. He is now a regular TV pundit for Sky Sports.

Best career advice
My headmaster said at my first school assembly: 'You will only get out of this school what you put into it.' Not a bad piece of advice.

He was also a cricket fan and would often come to watch the first eleven. The year I was captain I went out to toss. He asked me what I had decided to do. I said that I had decided to bat, but was worried whether it was the right decision or not. He then gave me another piece of excellent advice: 'Michael, the decision has been made. All you can do now is set about making sure it is the right one.'

What single piece of career advice would you give?
As above. Also, you must do something you enjoy. This is the first consideration – not the money or the prestige of the position.

What personal characteristics do you look for in others?

- They would have to fit in – get on with the people already employed or in the team.
- They would have to want the position.
- I would like to see them demonstrating responsibility and enthusiasm.

David Platt

David Platt proved himself a highly talented footballer, playing for such famous clubs as Aston Villa, Bari, Juventus, Sampdoria and Arsenal. During his playing career he scored over 200 first-class goals, claimed more than 60 England caps and was England Captain for three years. On retiring as a player he became Manager of Nottingham Forest and is now Manager of the England Under 21 team.

Best career advice
Continue to work hard and once you have made a decision, make the decision work.

What single piece of career advice would you give?
As above.

What personal characteristics do you look for in others?
Personality, confidence, belief.

Dickie Bird MBE

A talented young cricketer, Dickie Bird batted for Yorkshire and Leicestershire before becoming one of England's most respected and best-loved umpires. His career spanned 150 international matches, including a record 68 tests.

Best career advice
Work hard at what you are going to do. Show mental strength and, above all, believe in yourself.

What single piece of career advice would you give?

As above, believe in yourself. Mental strength is so important. You can have all the ability in the world, but if you do not believe in yourself, you will fall by the wayside.

What personal characteristics do you look for in others?

Honesty, fairness and character. Also, having a big smile on your face.

Part II

Taking Action

Chapter **8**

Advertised Openings

Advertised vacancies provide one of the most obvious sources for finding a potential new job. So how do you maximize your chances of making this route work for you?

The press

Advertising job vacancies in newspapers is an established recruitment technique the world over. In the USA, jobs of all types and levels of seniority are included in the classified ads sections. In the UK, the 'classifieds' tend to include more junior roles, whereas management positions will be presented in a display format.

Either way, looking through these job adverts gives you a sense of levels of current demand in the job market and the particular skills that employers are seeking. With luck, you will also spot the job that is just right for you.

Most national papers have pages of job ads. Sometimes the theme of these ads is linked to the theme of a supplement published that day. Some may have a daily theme focusing on a particular sector or type of job. For example, the *Guardian* publishes a media section on Monday, accompanied by pages of media and creative job ads. The *Financial Times* includes finance-related job adverts on a Thursday, when it also publishes an accountancy column.

The trade press aimed at your industry or profession also provides a highly targeted source of advertised vacancies. The journals and magazines of professional bodies also carry job ads. Get into the habit of looking regularly through all these sources.

Now to dispel a major myth. Some people feel there is no point answering an ad in a national newspaper such as the *Financial Times* because they believe it will attract hundreds or even thousands of responses.

Wrong!

Most ads in the *Financial Times*, for example, might on average attract around 100 responses, although there are variations. Responses to the trade press or financial journals will often be considerably smaller, sometimes just a handful. In general, experience shows that the higher the salary stated in the advert, the more the responses received.

Whatever the reality of any particular job advert, many people just assume there will be so many replies that they won't have a chance and so don't bother applying. They effectively self-select themselves out of the post.

Internet jobsites

The world of the Internet continues to expand into all areas of life. The realm of the job-hunter is no exception. Internet jobsites can provide a valuable source of advertised vacancies.

This is particularly true in technology-based sectors. If you are an IT consultant or programmer, you would be cutting yourself off from a huge source of working opportunities if you left these online recruiting sites untouched. However, even non-techie roles are now well-represented by online jobsites.

There are three main types of Internet jobsite:

- websites run by traditional offline recruitment consultancies;
- general sites, which are similar in nature to traditional newspaper 'classified' ads; and
- more specialized job websites, which focus on specific job disciplines.

Traditional consultancies

Traditional recruitment consultancies are increasingly advertising the positions they are currently engaged to fill on their own websites. By logging on regularly you should be able to get a good feel for the current state of market demand.

However, just as if you were using recruitment consultancies' resources in a traditional offline way, you will probably need to keep your eye on several sites to make sure you fully cover the sector of the job market relevant to you.

General jobsites

Huge generalist Internet jobsites (such as monster.com, stepstone.com or gojobsite.co.uk) can be useful for those job-seekers considering a wide range of career options, since you will be able to browse through a wide range of different jobs in different sectors in one place.

On the downside, if you do know precisely what you want, you need to make sure the jobsite's search engine is sufficiently finely tuned to enable you to find any jobs that meet your criteria. It can be frustrating and time-consuming if your search repeatedly throws up jobs that don't quite fit what you are looking for.

Specialists

The third type of online jobsite is offered by smaller specialists, or aggregators, who pull together the jobs being handled by recruitment consultancies within specialist industry sectors. Alan Dickinson, founder and Chief Executive of aggregator site jobs-financial.com, explains the concept:

> We specialize in the accountancy recruitment market and what we do is fairly typical. We sell advertising space to as many recruitment consultancies as we can within the discipline. This means we have a smaller number of jobs on our board compared to the huge generalists, but they are all within accounting. Rather than the individual having to go to each individual consultant's website they can view them all through one portal, which is a lot more straightforward for the candidate. The ease of searching for the job you want is substantially improved. It enables a more targeted search.

Online advantages

Using the Internet jobsites can be a highly efficient use of the job-seeker's time. You can get a good feel for the state of the recruitment market – the types of openings available and the skills in demand. As long as you have private access to the Internet you can search in your own time, at your own pace and be fully in control of what you look for; you can be as indiscriminate or as selective as you like. Best of all, you should be able to do this without having to leave any confidential information about yourself behind.

Clearly, things change, so it's worth keeping your eyes open for new online recruiters' sites opening up. It might be worth running occasional searches and keeping your eyes open for advertising flagging up a site you haven't seen before. Major generalist jobsite providers will run national TV or billboard advertising campaigns. Smaller specialists or aggregators will advertise in professional journals or trade press, so you should be able to find someone focused on your sector by flicking through relevant publications. You could also have a look at the website of the Association of Online Recruiters, details of which are given in the Appendix, to find a list of its members' names.

Corporate websites

Individual corporate websites also increasingly advertise current vacancies within the organization. If you have identified a number of preferred employers, who happen to be major organizations, then have a look to see whether they do this. If they do, you can quickly see whether what you have to offer is what they might be looking for.

As well as any positions currently needing to be filled, the websites often include current employee profiles. These give you a good feel of the prevailing corporate culture and the types of personalities who fit in well within it.

Responding effectively

How you reply to an advertised vacancy may differ slightly depending on whether it appears in the hard print press or on an Internet website, but there are some general principles to apply:

- Read the wording of the ad carefully.
- Tailor your CV to directly highlight the skills requested in the ad.
- Write a covering letter that emphasizes three or four of your key relevant attributes.
- Send your CV in within a week of the ad appearing if possible, and certainly within two weeks.

Check the wording

The job ad is trying to get across the employer's need succinctly. You need to be able to interpret the shorthand style to understand whether you can fit the bill, and how you should tailor your response.

Key issues to look out for when interpreting job adverts:

- **The employer is not named**
  This may be because the individual currently holding the advertised post does not know that they are to be replaced. Alternatively, the recruiter may want to include a salary figure in the advert, but salary is a sensitive issue due to internal politics. Another reason could be that the recruiting organization has recently received some bad press and decided not to reveal its name initially so as not to put applicants off.

- **Descriptions of the organization**
  'The company has experienced extremely rapid growth': this may mean that corporate systems haven't been able to cope with the pace of expansion and the company is a fairly anarchic place in which to work.
  Any reference to 'following a recent restructuring' may mean the company recently laid staff off.
  If a multinational refers to 'our recent merger', be warned that there may still be a fair amount of internal politics going on.

- **Imprecise location details**
  A general description such as 'in the South East' suggests a fairly remote or less popular location.

- **Imprecise job descriptions**
  The less precise the job description, the less 'sexy' it is probably perceived to be. For example, finance professionals may turn their noses up at 'an internal audit' role, so the employer may describe this instead as 'a critical financial role' to encourage more replies.

- **Features of the job**
  Ads may say a role 'involves a significant amount of travel': does this mean extended periods in a few locations overseas, or repeated day trips to attend meetings in foreign airport hotels? Remember the travel may not be to glamorous locations.

- **The person specification**
  Job adverts will generally describe the qualities sought in candidates. Interpret these carefully: 'resilience' may mean you will need to be tough because the employer's culture is a highly aggressive or competitive one; 'the ability to influence others':

a lot of selling could be involved; 'a high degree of computer-literacy': if this seems unnecessary for the job being advertised, it may mean the line manager is an IT and email fan.

- **The way the salary package is described**
  The advert may talk about a 'package worth £80k'. This is very different from offering a salary of £80,000. The package may include a car, pension contribution and other benefits, with a basic salary of just £40,000. When a salary says circa, that usually means there could be a variation of 10 to 15 per cent either way, depending on the age and experience of the successful applicant.

In general, the more hard facts there are included in the advert, the better; less openness and more imprecision suggests that the employer has something to hide. If the advert looks as though it has been designed with care, the employer is demonstrating

---

Commercial Accountant

Competitive package
South East

Our client is a long-established and highly respected organization, with a broad product range across a variety of industry sectors. Following a recent restructuring we are looking for an experienced finance professional to assist the newly appointed Finance Director in championing the change process.

This is an excellent opportunity for a highly commercial, qualified accountant to make a significant contribution to a rapidly developing operation at a critical phase of its development. You will need to be a strong manager, able to motivate teams of auditors across a variety of locations. With first-class influencing skills and the ability to communicate financial data clearly to non-financial managers, you will be tenacious with an appetite for hard work and a high level of commitment. Equally vital will be a track record of working within blue chip multinationals – gained either within industry or a major accounting firm.

In return we offer an excellent remuneration package and outstanding career development opportunities across a business that recognizes and rewards success.

Please send a full CV, enclosing details of current remuneration package to GKW Executive Selection,
16 Hamilton Street, St James's, London W1.

Figure 8.1 A sample job advert

its willingness to invest in its recruitment processes; that may mean it values its employees more than other employers who are content with more slapdash adverts.

What is the advert in Figure 8.1 really saying?

- **Job title**
  Does this reflect the true commercial nature of the role? Does the job really involve close working with the marketing department, or are they merely trying to 'hype' the role?

- **No salary indication given**
  Perhaps the recruiting company is concerned about pay comparabilities and is having to offer more than existing staff receive to attract the right sort of person; or perhaps merely stating 'competitive package' is designed to obscure the fact that the package is *not* actually that competitive.

- **Vague location**
  Is the company situated in an unattractive area?

- **No company identified**
  Has it had bad press or is the appointment highly confidential, i.e. is the current incumbent being replaced?

- **Woolly description of the company**
  Is it in a declining sector?

- **No financial figures given**
  Are their results unimpressive?

- **Recent restructure and new financial director**
  This probably means lots of change within the company, which could either create opportunity or instability.

- **'Strong manager ... strong motivational and influencing skills'**
  Is morale at rock bottom, or do they recognize the importance of leadership in the company?

- **Focus on 'communicating financial data to non-finance managers'**
  Is the business run by people with little interest in or respect for the finance function or is the work environment based on strong communication and close collaboration?

- **'Appetite for hard work' and 'high level of commitment'**
  This could mean long hours, or it could suggest the employer recognizes the importance of drive and determination in achieving career success.

All advertising can be misleading. Remember, the employer is trying to promote the job in order to attract the best candidates. As a candidate, you require as much hard information as possible. If the advert is unclear, try to find out more precise information from the recruitment consultancy involved.

Tailor your CV

If you have directly relevant experience, don't be put off if you don't quite meet all the requirements listed in the job advert. For example, if an advertisement says the employer is looking for a graduate, that isn't necessarily always the case; this is shorthand for 'graduate calibre'. However, you must make an effort to tailor your CV to highlight the ways you do meet the job specification.

We discussed the importance of preparing a suitable CV in Chapter 6, Preparing Your Marketing Material, but it's worth recapping a few key points. You don't want to waste your time and the recruiter's by sending in a standard CV that doesn't directly relate your skills to those of the job advertised. You must make the effort to adjust your CV to reflect your interpretation of what the recruiter is looking for.

Say the ad states that responsibilities will include managing staff, developing computer systems and running a multi-site activity. The ability to manage change is also desired. You must ensure that each of these requirements is addressed in your CV, referring to specific examples.

The covering letter

As we said in Chapter 6, the covering letter is one of the most underutilized tools in the job-hunting game. If you can make yours stand out from the crowd, you can significantly increase the chances of your CV attracting the recruiter's attention.

In your covering letter you should:

- pick out three or four key strengths or aspects of your experience that highlight your suitability for the advertised role and flag these up in the covering letter;

- include clear examples that demonstrate these strengths;
- specify clearly the job applied for and where you saw it advertised; and
- be concise.

Respond promptly

Most adverts will not specify a closing date for applications. However, you should aim to respond within a week if possible and certainly within ten days of the ad appearing.

Headhunter Suzzane Wood, Partner with executive search consultants Odgers Ray & Berndtson, says:

> I tell corporate clients that within two weeks of a job ad appearing I will come and see them with a list of candidates for consideration, who I plan to interview. However, if a candidate can respond within a week, that's great. Sooner rather than later is better. The world of recruitment is speeding up.

Kickstart Tip

Responding quickly doesn't mean, however, that you must rush your CV straight onto a fax to get it onto the recruiter's desk within an hour. You won't gain any advantage by doing this. On the contrary, by not taking the time to tailor your CV, you run the risk that it won't be sufficiently relevant to the particular vacancy.

The recruiter will gather together the applications received in response to an advert as they arrive. After perhaps a week, the process of reviewing the applications will begin, the aim being to whittle them down to a shortlist to invite for interview. If a recruitment consultancy has placed the ad, the consultant will typically be looking to interview a maximum of 12 people, from which perhaps just three or four will then be recommended for a further interview with the recruiting company. If the recruiting company is managing the process, it may seek an even smaller number for interview.

Either way, both will usually have a target number of people they intend to interview. If your application arrives after they have already picked the 12 interviewees they require to meet that target, you will find it that much harder to make it into the interview pile. In fact, you will need to be absolutely and obviously outstanding.

Internet-based and email responses

If you are replying to an advert on an Internet jobsite or corporate website, you will almost certainly be responding by email. As discussed in Chapter 6, Preparing Your Marketing Material, you can attach your CV in an appropriate file type (such as Word), so that makes no difference to the way you prepare your CV or its style and format. Your hard-copy covering letter is replaced by a covering email that follows the same principles – highlighting three or four specific reasons why you are worth considering for the vacancy.

Job fairs

Alongside advertised vacancies in the traditional press or on the Internet, job fairs provide a venue where a large number of recruiters will be gathered together specifically to recruit new employees. They can therefore provide an efficient opportunity for finding out information about a number of different organizations and of putting yourself forward as a possible candidate for their vacancies.

However, most of the vacancies will be at relatively low levels within the recruiting organizations – up to junior or middle management positions. This means that job fairs may be helpful for younger people or graduates, but they are not suitable hunting grounds for people seeking senior management roles.

Kickstart Tip

If you think a job fair may be useful for you, then treat your attendance with the same degree of seriousness as you would a meeting with a recruitment consultancy or an interview with an employer. This means you should dress just as smartly.

If you know that a couple of organizations that interest you will be present, make sure you have done your homework on them so that you have relevant questions to ask. You want to take every opportunity to impress them with your skills and potential.

You should expect to come away with a pile of information on a number of organizations, their products, services and vacancies. If you have registered your interest in any current vacancies, this material will be helpful should you subsequently be called for an interview.

Chapter summary: key points

- Advertised vacancies are a key resource for the job-hunter.
- Identify which national newspapers publish appropriate job ads on which days, as well as looking through the adverts in relevant professional or trade press.
- Don't self-select yourself out of the running by imagining adverts attract thousands of replies; they don't. If you are at all interested, apply.
- Keep an eye out for appropriate Internet jobsites, both general and specifically focused on your employment sector.
- When responding to an advert, read it carefully and try to understand what it is really saying.
- Make sure you tailor your CV to respond to the particular features of the job specification.
- Use your covering letter effectively to attract the recruiter's attention.
- Aim to reply to an advert within a week of its appearing.
- Respond to an Internet job ad via email, attaching your CV as a Word file.
- Job fairs may provide access to multiple employers seeking staff at relatively junior levels.
- If you attend a job fair, dress smartly, ask intelligent questions and aim to come away with plenty of information on attractive employers and new contact names.

Chapter 9

Following Through

You have seen your ideal job. You know you are perfect for it. You have assessed the key skills and personal characteristics specified in the job advert and believe you have them all. You have tailored your CV to highlight all your relevant experience and you have written an eye-catching covering letter that flags up your three or four key selling points. Now what do you do?

Following up the CV with a call

Mistakes do happen – even in recruiting. Your CV may be perfect and you may indeed be the ideal person for the position, but for some reason you slip through the net. Maybe your letter gets put on the wrong desk, is lost in the internal mail or simply doesn't get read because the recruiter made a mistake and put it in the rejection pile without properly reviewing it. Disaster!

Now wind back the tape. Go back in time. You know you are right for the job and expect to be called for an interview, but you don't want to leave anything to chance. What you can do is ring up the recruiter after you have sent in your CV, but before you expect the final shortlist of interviewees will have been drawn up.

This approach has several advantages. First, you can avoid losing out on your ideal job simply because someone (be it the post service, the internal post room or the recruiter) cocked up. Second, it gives you an additional chance to make yourself noticed.

Plan the call

You need to plan your call carefully, including the time of day that you ring. Your aim is to speak directly to the individual responsible for reviewing the applications for your target job. So you need to time your phone call to maximize your chances of speaking to that person directly. Say the advert you have responded to was placed by a recruitment consultancy. Recruitment consultants work long hours and tend to have strong defences – in the form of receptionists, PAs and secretaries who will intercept any calls made to them during normal working hours.

Kickstart Tip

You want to speak directly to the recruiter, not the PA, so this means you should time your call for outside standard working hours. If you phone early in the morning – before 8.30 a.m. – or after the end of standard office hours – say after 6 p.m. – you have a much greater chance of getting through to the individual recruiter.

Now, assume you have planned your campaign and dialled the recruiter's offices at the end of the day. You are put through to your target and then what? If you haven't prepared what to say, you could actually blow your chances by coming over badly on the phone. So – here comes one of the key rules for successful job-hunting again – make sure you prepare!

Think about the call as if it is a three-minute interview. You have won yourself three minutes to sell yourself and make sure that your CV gets into the 'interview definites' pile.

How not to do it

Try to avoid the disastrous impact made by one candidate who phoned up a recruiter handling an advertised vacancy. This caller clearly hadn't thought through the purpose of his call.

'Can I speak to Jeff Grout, please?'
'Speaking.'
'Ah, um, I'm phoning about the financial manager's job at BigCo plc. Could you tell me more about it, please?'
'What would you like to know?'
'Oh, well, who does the manager report to?'
'You should see from the advert we placed that the manager reports to the financial director.'
'Oh, yes. Where is the job based?'
'The head office is in Surrey and the distribution centre is in Birmingham, as I think you should again see from the ad.'

'Right. What about the salary package?'

'We said, in the ad, that it's negotiable around £45,000 per year.'

'OK. Well, thanks.'

'No problem.'

Clunk.

Actually there was a problem. The applicant had created an impression of being someone who was unable to pick out clearly stated information from an advert. He had made an impression, but one that ensured he did not make it onto the interview candidate shortlist. His CV went in the bin.

How to do it

So how should you make such a call? Think back to the covering letter you sent with your CV. The letter picked out three or four of your key attributes and highlighted them. The phone conversation should try to do the same, except that you will probably identify just one key selling point and focus on that. You want to elaborate how this characteristic, this particular experience you have, makes you suitable for the job and a definite interview candidate. Let's run that phone conversation again.

'Can I speak to Jeff Grout, please?'

'Speaking.'

'Jeff, hello. Sorry to trouble you at the end of the day.'

'No problem. How can I help?'

'Well, I appreciate you have probably had a large response to your recent advertisement for a financial manager position at BigCo plc.'

'Yes, we have.'

'I thought I would call you because I feel strongly that the systems experience I have is directly suited to the position.'

'I see. Why is that?'

'Well, I noted from the advertisement that the position calls for someone with management experience in systems implementation. My current company has just finished implementing a new accounts system across a number of locations. I was closely involved in choosing the package and then managing the implementation process, coordinating with our IT department on the timing of the implementa-tion. I made sure the finance team's work was not unduly interrupted and also ensured that a number of tailored applications were added, one of which has enabled us to derive more relevant management information on our distribution function. We have since improved speed of delivery in response to orders by 20 per cent.'

'That is interesting because my client is hoping to improve the performance of its distribution function. Look, I don't have much time to talk now but give me your name again. Have you already sent in your application?'

'Yes, I have. My name's Peter Bolton.'

'Good. Well, I'll certainly make sure we've got your details and I'll look through your CV. But on the face of it, you sound extremely suitable for the position. We'll be arranging interview times shortly so you can expect to hear from us in the next week or so. If you haven't heard anything in ten days, please give me another ring.'

'That's great, Jeff. Thanks for your time.'

Clunk.

The recruiter doesn't mind giving up that kind of time. The call has reassured him that there is indeed a potentially highly suitable candidate out there and one with the get-up-and-go to find the right job. An articulate candidate too. That CV will be in the interview pile immediately, after the briefest of scans for any obvious flaw that would rule the candidate out.

If you decide to make such a phone call, you might also want to prepare one or two cunning questions about the job, *on issues that aren't covered in the ad*. These should show the depth of your knowledge of the industry or the likely job role. They could be about the computer systems used in the department, the number of people who would be reporting to you, the potential for travel or the opportunities for commercial decision-making. Try to think of questions that link in some way to the experience you have. For example, if you are asking about the commercial decision-making potential of the role, you want to be able to drop into the conversation the fact that you recently devised the budget for a new promotional campaign and helped to select which prod-ucts should be included in the promotion.

Above all, focus on trying to spark the recruiter's interest. You want your name to be remembered so that it leaps out of the CV pile.

Monitoring results

As you proceed through the job application process, you might want to establish a system for capturing key data at each stage and for monitoring your results.

For example, each time you apply to an advertised vacancy, you need to keep a copy of:

- the job advert itself;
- your tailored CV; and
- your covering letter.

If you are applying to several jobs simultaneously, you can easily become confused about what particular attributes you emphasized in which application. You want to have the information readily to hand so that you can remind yourself of key details before an interview.

Kickstart Tip

You might also want to maintain a summary sheet, perhaps stapled to your copy of the job advert, which records the progress of your application.

For example, if you phone a recruiter after sending in an application, make a note of the call details: who you spoke to, on what date, any information you learned about the appointment or recruitment process and any necessary follow-up action. When you attend an interview, make a note of the interviewers' names and anything useful you find out from them.

Handling rejection

If you are looking for your ideal job, and if you are setting yourself challenging career goals, then you are likely to face rejection along your job-hunting journey. Rejection can be particularly hard to stomach if you have been out of work for some time; each rejection letter you receive can sap your determination to continue just that little bit more. In Chapter 4 we looked at ways to keep up your morale during the job hunt. Remember: try to keep focusing on your goal – your ideal job and a fulfilling career. The next application you make could be the one that hits home.

Making the most of feedback

When job-hunting you have to remember that, in most cases, the CVs you send speculatively to potential employers will not result in a job for you. That is normal and to be expected. Nor should it matter to you because all you need is one CV to reach the right person in the right organization at the right time.

Kickstart Tip

Let's say you sent a CV speculatively, but have heard nothing back in ten days. Don't ignore it. You should follow it up with a phone call, just as if you had responded to a publicized vacancy.

Just as we discussed above, you need to prepare what you intend to say before picking up the phone. You should be well briefed about the organization and how you think you could add value to it, because this knowledge is what triggered the speculative approach in the first place. Your aim is to check that the CV was received, to remind the targeted recipient of your existence, and to try to establish some rapport over the phone.

The answer you receive may be that there is simply nothing suitable for you with the employer at the present time. Don't just hang up the phone at this point. You might gain some useful information by continuing the conversation a little further. You could:

- ask for any comments on your CV and whether there was any other useful information you could have added;
- enquire whether there is likely to be some potential openings suitable for you in future; and
- ask whether the individual knows of anyone else in the organization or outside it who might have need for your expertise.

Remember, there is never any harm in asking polite questions. Ideally you want to end the conversation with a new name and number of someone you can contact. This could be the lead that results in an interview with your preferred employer.

The interview: learning from your mistakes

Say your speculative application or your response to an advertised vacancy won you the desired interview. Fantastic!

But then you don't get called back for a second interview. Or you make it to the final shortlist, but you don't ultimately receive the job offer.

You will inevitably feel disappointed and maybe even hurt. This is natural, but unhelpful. You need, where possible, to develop an attitude that treats each interview as an opportunity to practise your interview skills.

Kickstart Tip

To make the most of the experience, you could follow up your interview with a letter or phone call asking for feedback. Were there any particular areas that let you down? What were your strongest points? This is useful information that you can use to your advantage next time.

The more ready you are to learn from your experiences, the greater your chances of landing your dream job in future.

Contacting the employer again

Depending how your job search goes, you might also want to contact the organization again perhaps three to six months after your interview. If you made it onto the shortlist of candidates and believe you did reasonably well at your final interview, then you can feel pretty confident that the organization likes what you have to offer.

Kickstart Tip

Contacting the employer again a few months later could be helpful to them, and to you. It may well be that the successful candidate, who was originally offered the job, didn't actually fit in and is now on the point of leaving. Perhaps someone else in the department, who was hoping for promotion into that role, has just resigned and is on the point of leaving. Maybe this is a role that would also be suitable for you.

Your phone call or letter could enable the employer to fill the imminent job gap without having to go through the whole recruiting process all over again. By getting in touch again you could be saving them a lot of time and trouble, and boosting your career at the same time.

Chapter summary: key points

- Following up your CV with a phone call to the recruiter can avoid job-hunting disasters where your application is mistakenly overlooked.
- If you impress the recruiter, you can improve your chances of being invited to an interview.
- In order to impress, prepare what to say and stress one major personal attribute relevant to the job.
- Don't ask questions the job advert has already answered.
- Ask intelligent questions which reveal your knowledge and experience.
- Keep relevant information related to the job application together so you can refer to it easily.
- Record your progress, including details of any phone calls and interview outcomes.
- Don't be put off by rejection.
- If your CV doesn't result in an interview, try to find out why.
- Use any such phone call to try to find out about other potential vacancies.
- If your interview doesn't land you the desired job, write and ask for feedback on your performance.
- The sooner you learn from your mistakes, the sooner you should land your ideal job.
- If you believe you were close to success at a final interview, contact the organization again in a few months' time; circumstances change and your services might now be required.

Chapter 10

Making the Most of Recruitment Consultancies

Some job-hunters may find their interests effectively served by signing up with a specialist recruitment firm. This way you can gain access to known career opportunities and tap into specialist expertise on the job market.

Why use a recruitment consultancy?

If you are serious about finding a job or giving your career a boost, then you almost certainly want to register with some kind of recruitment consultancy or agency. In fact if you don't, you are likely to miss out on a large number of openings, because the vast majority of vacancies are actually handled by third-party recruitment firms.

Kickstart Tip

Recruitment specialists are also an invaluable source of advice and market information. They can give you an idea of the type of salary you might expect in a new job, taking into account prevailing market conditions. They can advise you on which of your particular skills are likely to be most attractive to employers. You can ask for advice on whether your CV presents you in the best light.

As you start applying for positions, the consultants can also provide you with background information about the client company. And since the client company is paying the consultancy for handling the vacancy, all these services come to you for free.

However, recruitment firms do differ in style and in the types of openings they are engaged to fill. So if you are thinking of using one, make sure it's the right type for you.

Inside the recruitment industry: headhunters, consultancies and agencies

There used to be clear delineation between different types of recruitment specialist firm. At the top end were the headhunters – or executive search specialists. These firms never advertised vacant positions. They focused their energies purely on senior level positions, which they filled by a search activity – utilizing research to identify suitable candidates doing similar work in rival or complementary organizations.

Then there were the selection consultancies. These firms would be engaged by a client organization to place an advertisement in appropriate media. They would then select and shortlist suitable candidates from the pool of applicants who responded to the ad. Consultancies offered a certain level of advice to client companies about how they should fill their vacant positions, therefore justifying the use of the word 'consultancy'.

Finally came the recruitment agencies, which tended simply to maintain a database of potential job-seekers, but offered little in the way of consultancy advice.

Nowadays the boundaries between these different types of organization are becoming increasingly blurred. Headhunters increasingly advertise some of the positions they are engaged to fill. Similarly, some selection consultancies now conduct executive searches to find particular high-level appointments. Many such search and selection firms also maintain databases, often filled using the responses received to job advertisements. Meanwhile, a number of recruitment agencies place adverts and conduct selection work using the responses these generate, as well as conducting occasional search activity.

Choosing the right one for you

Your choice of recruitment specialist will be determined for you if you are responding to a job advertisement. If you are seriously looking for a job move and replying to a number of different advertisements simultaneously, you can easily find yourself on the databases of a number of different consultancies.

However, if you decide to talk to a recruitment firm directly, you must check in advance that you are targeting the right people. You need to find a firm that specializes in your sector, at your level, with an impressive client list and a high success rate in placing candidates.

Obtaining a personal recommendation from someone you know who has moved jobs in your sector with the help of a recruitment firm is one of the best ways of making your choice. However, if you don't have any such recommendations and don't already know the names of recruitment firms specializing in your sector, a glance at the job adverts in appropriate trade and professional press should give you some leads. In addition, *Executive Grapevine*, a published directory of all types of recruitment organization, will give you an exhaustive list (see the Appendix for details). If you think the directory might help, look for it in the library, as it is rather expensive to buy. However, because so many firms are listed, the vast majority won't be relevant to your circumstances. Be focused in your choices.

You can also find names of recruiters through the Recruitment and Employment Confederation (REC) and its specialist divisions, such as the Association of Search and Selection Consultants. By using the REC's website you can also find links through to recruitment consultancies' websites, which will give you an idea of how suitable they are for your requirements (see Appendix for contact details).

Once you have identified some potentially suitable firms you should ask them a number of key questions, just to ensure they are the right people to use for your job hunt.

Questions to ask could include:

- Does the firm specialize in your sector?
- What level of seniority does it concentrate on?
- What is the average salary range for the jobs it handles?
- What client organizations does it work for?
- Which of these does it represent exclusively?
- How many people does it place per month?
- What proportion of candidates are placed within three months?

On the subject of client names, maintain a degree of healthy scepticism when firms say they work for x, y and z plcs. At middle management level, many major organizations use a number of recruitment firms simultaneously. You might want to find out whether the recruitment firm has a formal agreement with the client organization, which gives it exclusivity in handling the client's recruitment affairs.

You could try asking to speak to a number of people the recruitment firm has placed successfully. However, they may be wary of agreeing to this. It should, however, be possible to ask to see testimonials from happy customers.

How many consultancies to use

When choosing a recruitment firm, it's probably worth registering with between three and five organizations. Although there will probably be some duplication in terms of the clients they serve, there will be variations at the edges. If you are about to be made redundant, your employer is on the verge of going bankrupt, or you are open to a broad range of job possibilities, then your best bet probably will be to get a number of recruitment firms on your case immediately.

However, a firm may try to persuade you to give it a period of exclusivity so that you don't sign up with a number of its rivals. There are some situations where this may be worth considering for a limited period – for example, if you don't want to be inundated with multiple interviews or if you are particularly concerned with confidentiality.

Of course, if you agree to exclusivity for a certain period you need to be confident in the abilities of the potential firm to help you. Your decision should be influenced not only by the firm's track record, but also by the rapport you develop with the particular consultant you meet. If the consultant appears to understand your needs, expresses enthusiasm and confidence that your aims can be fulfilled and you feel a degree of trust developing between you, it may be reasonable to agree to use that firm alone for perhaps a month or two. If the service fails to deliver, you can always review the situation.

How to get consultancies on your side

It is common to hear people who have used a recruitment agency moaning about aspects of the service they received:

'The consultant was slow to return my calls.'

'They didn't come up with anything for weeks.'

'I couldn't get an interview to discuss my needs.'

These complaints are sometimes justified, but they frequently result from misconceptions about the role of the recruitment consultant and the service they actually provide.

When dealing with a recruitment consultant, you are more likely to develop a positive relationship if you remember the stresses and drivers that apply. You should understand that:

- consultancies find people for jobs, not jobs for people;
- the corporate client pays the bills and takes precedence over the candidate's needs;
- you receive advice and help for free; and
- time is money – you should try not to waste the consultant's time.

Having said all that, if you have skills in demand, then you are a valuable commodity to the consultant and should expect to be treated with courtesy and professionalism.

The initial approach

You might think that having selected a suitable recruitment consultancy, all you have to do is phone up and the consultant you speak to will be dying to get you in for a chat. That is not necessarily so. In fact, the more senior you are, the more difficult you may find it to attract a consultancy's interest.

This may seem odd, but think about it. At lower management levels, say that of a newly qualified accountant, there are lots of jobs and lots of employers fighting for the same people. You are in demand. The higher up the managerial food chain you rise, the fewer the jobs and proportionately the more people available to fill them.

The reality is that, in most situations and most recruitment firms, the consultant won't actually be that keen to meet you. Unless there is a pressing job to fill, meeting you only takes their time away from fulfilling a client's immediate needs.

If you remember that the consultant will be trying to meet the brief set by a corporate client, and that you are only of interest if you potentially could fill that brief, then you are more likely to get the response you want.

Getting a foot in the consultancy's door

Your first challenge when contacting a consultancy is to make the consultant willing to meet you. There are a number of ways that you can increase your chances. These include:

- making sure you have picked an appropriate consultancy in the first place;
- calling someone you have a connection with; and
- express your willingness to fit in with the consultant's timetable.

We have already talked about the importance of choosing an appropriate recruitment firm.

Kickstart Tip

If you have been given a recommendation by someone recently placed in a similar sector and position to you, make the most of that contact. Tell the consultant that your friend recommended the firm and their particular services, and that you believe you too could be suitable for some of the positions they are likely to be handling.

Even better, if one of your contacts is a personal friend of a suitable recruitment consultant, ask this contact to call on your behalf. Any leverage that helps you get through the door is worth applying.

When you make contact, be polite and flexible. Offer to meet at the consultant's convenience, at a time that suits them, even if it's early in the morning or in the early evening when you would normally be on the train home. Make it clear you don't expect to take up too much time. Perhaps you could pop in for a 20-minute chat?

Building a relationship

You are far more likely to get positive results from using a recruitment firm if you put the effort into building a sound relationship with the consultants you meet.

Kickstart Tip

Remember, the initial meeting is a key opportunity for you to sell yourself to the consultant. You should treat that meeting, and any subsequent ones that you have, with the same attitude as if you were heading into a potential employer's office for an interview.

This relationship starts from the first phone call to arrange a meeting and develops from there. At the first meeting, consultants will form a number of impressions about you that could determine how positive they are about promoting you to one of their clients.

The consultant is, after all, acting as the employer's representative and making initial selections on the employer's behalf. Therefore, to get through to meet the employer, you need to impress the consultant.

The best way to do this is to:

- always arrive on time for meetings;
- dress as you would for a job interview – smartly;
- always be polite;
- focus on communicating your positive attributes;
- express enthusiasm for your job search; and
- try to build rapport as quickly as possible.

If you take this approach, the consultant will at least see you as someone likely to present themselves well in front of the client company.

For example, your appearance really is important. Just because it's summer and hot and you've taken a few days off work, that doesn't give you the excuse for sauntering into the consultancy's office in baggy shorts and a T-shirt. How does the consultant know that you won't be as casual when you are off for an interview with a client company? Don't give the consultant any reason to doubt your seriousness as a candidate.

Kickstart Tip

If the consultant likes you and believes you have an impressive personality, then you are even further ahead in the job-hunting game. The fact is that you may not have the greatest CV on earth. Maybe you feel you have been stagnating in your current role and haven't developed new skills recently. The consultant recognizes this. However, you express yourself well, have a positive attitude and a willingness to put in effort to develop any new skills required in a new job. You appear a sound pair of hands.

If you can get consultants to believe in you in this way, then they are more likely to stick their neck out and recommend you to the client. 'Look, Bob, I know this guy's CV doesn't look as hot as some. But I think you'll like him. He's got lots of character and is really ready for this kind of move. I think you'd find him committed and willing to put in the graft.' That's the kind of endorsement that gets you onto the interview shortlist, even if you don't quite meet the exact job specification.

Remember that consultants need to find candidates they can recommend to their client companies. They want you to do well. Treat them with respect, and the chances are they will do the same for you.

Attracting the headhunter's eye

Headhunters focus on the top, highest-profile jobs. If you want your career to have a real boost, attracting the headhunter's eye is certainly a good way of doing it.

You will clearly need to be in work and have a fair amount of experience under your belt. Sometimes the simple fact that you hold the job title you do may result in you getting called up by a headhunter. If this happens, even if you are not currently looking for a job move, try to be polite. This person may hold the key to your dream job in a few years' time.

However, if you aren't getting those tempting calls and you want to attract a headhunter's attention, you can take action to develop a higher profile in your industry or profession. You could do this by:

- speaking at conferences;
- writing articles; and
- publicizing job moves.

Chris Long, a partner with Whitehead Mann GKR, a senior executive search consultancy (also known as 'headhunters'), says:

> You want to make yourself easy to be identified as a potential candidate for a senior position; that's about raising your profile, building a reputation and seeking platforms to let people know who you are and what you have done within the company or the industry. It's about networking with the people that headhunters would naturally go to for recommendations. It's worth spending a percentage of

your time in your working life actively managing your career and developing your brand equity with the headhunting fraternity. You could try and stay well in with two of three select headhunters who are focused on your industry or specialism.

Conference speaking

The conference industry now hosts events that address a huge range of topics, on business, environmental, social, medical and legal issues, among many others. These conferences rely on able and willing speakers to cover current topical subjects. If you are contacted to speak, even if you don't really want to have to give up the time, it may be worth considering as a profile-raising move.

You could keep your eyes open for conferences being advertised in your trade or professional press. If you see topics recurring that you think you could speak on, you could call the organizers directly. Most subjects will be repeated at regular intervals. If you can use some work you have done in your organization as a case study, even better. If you become known as a speaker – a stimulating and informative one – then your name will start to be known in your industry.

Writing articles

Another approach is to offer to write articles for your trade or professional press, or even national newspapers. Many publications have some form of opinion section, which is filled weekly or monthly by different specialists – not journalists. As long as you have something interesting to say, this is again a way to bring yourself to the attention of your colleagues in the industry, and potentially of headhunters. You won't necessarily generate instant results, but over a relatively short period of time you could build up a useful reputation as a commentator on your sector.

Publicizing job moves

Although this may sound an illogical approach for attracting a headhunter, you could undertake a degree of self-promotion when you change jobs.

Kickstart Tip

Say you have just moved into a more senior role in a rival company. Most trade papers have a 'movers' section, which briefly reports on which people have recently changed roles or employers in the industry. If you can get your name and new role printed in a suitable publication, you could take a copy and send it to a firm of headhunters. You can attach a note that simply says, 'For your information, I have recently been appointed marketing director of x plc. I enclose my updated CV for your records.'

Clearly you are not looking for an immediate move at this point, but you are signalling to the headhunter that you are a potential mover and shaker, someone worth keeping an eye on who might be worth contacting in future. By the time the note in the press is published and you contact the headhunter you will have been in your new job for several months anyway. In just another year or 18 months you could well be ready for another move.

An unusual approach

Some people have occasionally been known to use a somewhat more devious method to useful effect. Say you are planning to leave your current employer in several months' time. Perhaps you know that there is a reorganization on the cards and your job is to be abolished. It has been known for such people to use the opportunity to phone a headhunter and tell them that a major reorganization is underway and their services may be required to fill new roles. The consultant comes in for a chat, sensing some lucrative assignment in the offing.

You have the perfect chance to show yourself in a positive light in your office environment. What you want to do is build up a rapport with the consultant quickly. You then inform the consultant that unfortunately your job is one of those now being restructured out of existence and therefore you are no longer actually in a position to appoint the recruiter's firm. However, you are clearly soon to be available should there be any suitable positions the consultant needs to fill.

Contacting headhunters directly

The headhunters' maxim is: 'Don't call us; we'll call you.' They pride themselves on their ability to source their own candidates by searching the marketplace.

That said, some are also open to direct approaches. In our survey, almost three-quarters of the headhunters said they would always read a speculative application and two-thirds said they would always respond to them. Many said they received such speculative approaches on a daily basis.

The majority of headhunters said that speculative applications would always be considered for current roles although less than half said they would consider speculative applications for forthcoming positions. In other words, your details won't necessarily be kept on file.

Temporary options

Some people wanting to kickstart their career might consider registering with recruitment agencies that specialize in temporary positions, as well as permanent ones. This is because temporary work can be an effective route into a permanent job.

Benefits of temporary work

There are several potential advantages of taking a temporary position. First, that short-term position can, sometimes, turn into a permanent one. This may happen because the person on maternity leave, for whom you are covering, decides not to come back. Or the interim departmental reorganization that created your role becomes fixed as it is. As far as the organization is concerned, it then has a choice – go out and spend time and money trying to recruit an unknown outsider, or offer the job to someone who has already proved their ability, who knows the ropes and can take over the permanent position with the minimum of internal disruption.

> ### Kickstart Tip
>
> This is why temping can be such a powerful route to permanent employment: it allows you the chance to showcase your skills.

Who is suited to temporary work?

The temping market has traditionally suited youngsters wanting to work for brief but intense periods before taking extended holidays to travel the world. It can also help people unsure about their next permanent career move; taking a string of short-term positions gives the temporary worker an insight into a far wider range of organizations more quickly than would be possible with a series of permanent roles.

However, temporary workers can be any age. In fact, people over 40 can find the permanent job market increasingly hard to crack as they come up against younger rival candidates, while in the temp world, age can be a definite advantage. You're more likely to have 'seen it all before' and have the confidence to walk into a role and take charge quickly.

People considering temporary work do need certain characteristics, however. You need to be able to cope with the uncertainty that you may not know what you will be doing in a week or two weeks' time. You also need the kind of personality that is happy joining an office team, getting to know people and then moving on again to a new, unfamiliar organization. Not everyone likes so much variation in their working relationships. However, if you are comfortable with repeated change, then taking temporary assignments can have a highly positive impact on your general outlook and the positivity with which you approach the job-hunting game.

Confidence booster

For people who have been out of work for a number of months, taking a temporary position can also help boost confidence, create a newly positive attitude and help to keep skills current.

If you are looking for a permanent job while filling a temporary one, you are more likely to give off the vibes of employability that employers look for – the energy, self-belief and focused attitude of mind. Think of the difference in your state of mind before and after a holiday. Before going away, most people work themselves up into a frenzy of activity – finishing off projects, tidying up loose ends, getting a lot done in a short period. When they come back, they are relaxed and refreshed, but generally take a little time to build up again into the swing of work. The same can happen when you have an extended period out of work. Temping helps to keep you tuned into workplace attitudes.

> ## Kickstart Tip
>
> Even people who have just left a permanent role, but one they have held for a long period of time, can find that taking a number of temporary positions can boost their CV. By working in a number of different environments in quick succession you gain exposure to a wider range of working practices and skills. You are demonstrating that you are employable currency.

Nor should temporary positions be associated with junior roles. High-level jobs can suddenly become vacant for unexpected reasons, causing a major organizational headache. One particular organization was looking to fill a £120,000-a-year role and had very fixed ideas about the kind of person who would be suitable – the likely age, experience and career history. This was a critical position that would become vacant very soon. The organization decided it had to take on a temporary individual to fill the role while they looked for a permanent replacement. The man they accepted on the temporary basis came nowhere near meeting all the attributes the employer had initially decided were necessary in the permanent employee. However, this individual had extremely good soft management skills, particularly in terms of communication and the ability to motivate the staff around him. After a couple of months in the role, the organization recognized his positive impact and offered him the position on a permanent basis.

Interim management

The interim manager is often seen as the ultimate high-level temp. However, specialists in interim placement tend to define the role more precisely.

Interim managers strictly speaking are required to handle particular situations – certain problems, projects or pressures – usually involving some kind of change management in an organization. This can be during a reorganization, in the period after an acquisition when two organizations are being fully integrated, or when an operating division is being closed down or sold off.

Because of the nature of these roles, interim managers are required to be senior, extremely experienced individuals used to taking decisions quickly and motivating the people around them. In contrast to the ordinary job market, grey hairs are a definite advantage. If you are to be considered suitable for an interim management role, you will need to have been through such a reorganization perhaps several times before and know the pitfalls and immediate challenges. You need to be able to walk into the role and make things happen fast.

To be an effective interim manager you also need to be:

- adaptable;
- able to absorb and analyse information quickly;
- an effective communicator;
- a good team player; and
- diplomatic and tactful.

Interim management is no soft option. It is in fact harder to be a good interim manager than a good manager. People who become interim managers generally do so because they are looking for new challenges, but don't want to be tied into a permanent job. They make a positive decision that this is the type of role they now want. The nature of the work is inevitably demanding and potentially stressful, but it is well paid.

If you think this kind of lifestyle might suit you, contact one of the specialist placement firms that focuses on interim management. Arrange a meeting to talk about whether you might have skills in demand in the marketplace.

Chapter summary: key points

- Registering with a recruitment consultancy can give you access to a wide range of jobs.
- Understand the services offered by the different types of recruitment specialist.
- Headhunters fill the most senior positions, mostly by seeking out high-flying individuals in the sector.
- Recruitment consultancies will advertise jobs, but may also conduct some head-hunting or search activities.
- Choose your recruitment consultancy on the basis of its sector focus, client list and record in placing candidates of your seniority level.
- Try to understand how recruitment consultancies operate and that their first loyalties are to their corporate clients who pay their bills.
- Try to fit your need for a meeting around the consultant's timetable.
- Remember you need to sell yourself to recruitment consultants.

- Getting a recruitment consultant on your side can help open doors to employers.
- You can take steps to attract the headhunter's eye – through conference-speaking, writing articles and publicizing your job moves.
- Taking temporary work can be an effective strategy for kickstarting your career.
- Temporary positions increase your range of experience in a short timescale.
- Sometimes temporary positions turn into permanent ones.
- Interim management can provide a rewarding career option for experienced, highly able managers looking for new challenges.

Chapter 11

Making Your Own Opportunities

When looking for your ideal job, advertised vacancies and recruitment consultancies are useful resources, but also obvious ones. The most innovative and therefore potentially most successful job-hunters put effort into making their own opportunities for career success.

Is an external move the best bet?

In many ways the most successful job move is one within your existing employer's organization. The inherent risks involved in moving to a new, unfamiliar organization have been stressed already. Your target employer may offer an impressive face to the external world and appear professional in its approach to your job application, but the reality of life in the firm may be quite different.

If your current employer is failing to meet your current requirements because it pays lower-than-average salaries, training and development are under-resourced and its prospects are uncertain, then you may have little to lose by moving elsewhere. But if your employer does pay well, provides training programmes and seems to be performing relatively well in its sector, you might think twice about your reasons for leaving.

Perhaps you want a different role. Or you want more pay and responsibility. What you would like, in fact, is a promotion.

Planning for promotion

The first step in achieving a promotion is to ask for it. This is also true if you decide you want to develop your skills laterally, by gaining more breadth in your role.

The simple rule – 'If you don't ask, you don't get' – certainly applies within organizations. Your manager won't necessarily be aware of your needs. In fact, managers may prefer, if unprompted, to keep their staff in their current positions because that makes for an easy life. If you move up, who will take your place? And who will have to spend time finding someone to fill your place? On the other hand, the organization as a whole should recognize that it has more to gain by keeping you than by letting you go over to the competition. Your manager may even have staff retention as one of their performance criteria determining next year's bonus.

So, take every opportunity to express your desire to progress and develop. Discuss potential options at any appraisals you have, or request a special meeting if you don't want to wait. Keep your eyes and ears open for any signs that your colleagues in slightly senior roles might be planning to move on soon. If their role is one you want, suggest being trained up so that promoting you to the role becomes the obvious decision.

But what if there are no openings in your particular department? You then need to consider whether any other departments in the organization might have an appropriate role. Contact the personnel department to discuss your needs. If they are unresponsive, think about what other direction you can take.

Kickstart Tip

If there is a particular department you think could be interesting, find out who the line manager is and try to book a meeting. It's always better to get your message across in person. Even if there is no suitable opening immediately, what if someone resigns in two weeks' time? You want your name to spring straight to mind.

Above all, remember that enthusiasm, motivation and a proactive approach can never damage your career. As the saying goes, 'There is no harm in asking.'

Changing direction? Consider an internal move

Internal moves can be particularly valuable if you have decided you want to change your career direction. Perhaps you started out training in the finance department but, two or three years on, you realize that you are far more interested in the marketing of products than in costing their production.

Persuading a new employer, who has no experience of your commitment, energy and creative thinking, to give you a marketing job will almost certainly be harder than persuading your current organization to let you transfer into a trainee marketing role. In fact, your employer could see the positive benefits for the marketing team in such a move. For example, you will be able to bring a sense of financial realism to the process of planning marketing promotions.

Clearly you will need to be able to put a convincing case for why it is in the organization's interests to help you switch; don't just focus on your own needs. Remember one of the guiding principles of the successful career – focus on what you can do for the organization, not on what the organization can do for you.

Networking personal contacts

If you decide you do need to look outside your current employer's organization in order to kickstart your career, make the most of networking opportunities.

> ### Kickstart Tip
>
> Personal networks are potentially the most productive, but most untapped, resource for job-hunters. By plugging into your personal contacts you immediately have access to people who know you and will want to help you. In fact, research tends to show that the more senior the position you want, the more likely you are to find it through networking than through any formal procedure such as responding to a job ad or using a recruitment consultancy.

This informal job market is therefore an essential area for you to investigate. So how do you go about it? First, don't be put off by the word 'networking'.

Networking for life, not just for a job

To some people, 'networking' can sound unpleasantly cold and calculating. It shouldn't. In its purest form the activity of networking is about responding to the people around you, picking up on what each individual has to offer and identifying shared characteristics, experiences or goals. When you express interest in talking to someone, when you find some mutual topic of conversation, you are immediately starting to build a relationship with them. If you are positive and friendly, they are likely to be positive and friendly back.

So networking is also about making friends. Some of the people you meet along the way – whether at school, college, in your first job, at your sister's wedding – may never be in a position to help your career. But they might well enrich your life.

Your network starts with your family as its foundation. Over time you will add, on top, new layers of intertwining relationships – from school, college, clubs, jobs, professional societies, friends of friends . . . Being an effective networker means you never close off the opportunity of adding a new name to your existing, ever-evolving contact book.

Effective networking for your career

Some people are natural networkers. They are good at 'working a room' at conferences; they remember people's names and keep in touch, formally or informally, with people they either feel a bond with or feel could be useful or interesting people to know. They stay in touch, however sporadically, with old colleagues or college friends. These natural networkers are already ahead in the career game because they will have a huge pool of names to dip into when researching new opportunities.

When you want to draw on your network to boost your career at a particular time, the first stage is to draw up a comprehensive list of *everyone* you know.

It is important to include *everyone*.

Kickstart Tip

Some people in your network may be more obviously able to help, but you don't want to start subconsciously editing anyone out and closing off any avenue at this stage.

The most common mistake that people make when asked to list their own network is that they write a list that is far too short. Because they are thinking about job-hunting, they tend only to think about people they know through business contact – people they have worked with or people they met on a course.

This is wrong. Your list should include:

- family – including uncles, aunts, cousins, step-sisters, etc.;
- friends – from school, university, social clubs;
- friends of friends – that person you sat next to at your best friend's barbecue last summer;
- work colleagues – past and present;
- your accountant or personal financial adviser;

- your neighbours;
- your bank manager; and
- everybody else who even vaguely knows you.

You might think including some of these people is a waste of time. How could the bank manager possibly be able to help with your desire to get a new job in advertising? Well, unknown to you, the bank manager's brother has worked with a successful recruitment consultancy for 15 years. So, to repeat, list everyone you can think of, everyone who appears in your personal universe, however rarely or remotely. Once you have drawn up your first list, let your subconscious continue to mull over your contacts and jot down new names whenever they come to you.

When you start contacting people, you should obviously start with those names you think most likely to be useful to you. But those lower down should never be discarded; you can never be sure just who will provide the lead that ultimately leads to your job-hunting success. Next, be clear about what you want to use these names for.

Using contacts effectively

> ### Kickstart Tip
>
> You are *not* listing the people in your network simply with a view to asking them whether they know of any jobs that are going. What you *do* want to do is to pick their brains for *information*: any insights they have into potential openings, industry developments and suggestions for other people you could speak to.

The way that you approach your contacts is also vital for determining how successful you are likely to be in getting the information you want. Where possible, try not to do most of your research over the phone. If your old college chum is now working in Aberdeen and you are based in Cornwall, then you probably have no option. However, the problem with using the phone is that it tends to make people focus their requests for help too narrowly. 'I'm phoning you because . . .' You may say you're trying to find a new job and your contact simply replies they can't help. That's a wasted contact.

Face-to-face contact

What you really want to do is to meet in person. Say the person you want to network is an old business contact. You aren't particularly close and any phone call is likely to last perhaps no more than 10 minutes. However, even the shortest face-to-face meetings tend to last at least half an hour. That gives you perhaps 20 extra minutes' worth of information from this contact. Face-to-face conversations also tend to be more elastic than phone conversations, heading off more easily into potentially productive tangents and generating new ideas for you to follow up. So, what you should try to do is arrange a meeting, but one that appreciates how precious is the time of the person you are contacting. You could suggest getting together over breakfast, coffee or lunch.

> ### Kickstart Tip
>
> Don't be afraid to say that you are looking for this person's help – most people are flattered by being asked for help – but make it clear you are not asking for work directly.
>
> This is important. Most people become nervous if they think you are asking for a job, or for them to recommend you to their own employer. If you are contacting a friend, they may feel you are confusing the boundaries of your relationship. So make it clear that what you are asking for is any information, insights or wisdom the person can give you that could help you advance your career or give you some new ideas for your job search. You want to talk about their sector, their competitors and key dynamics in the marketplace.

When you meet, the chances are that you will naturally talk about old mutual acquaintances. These may be names you have forgotten to include in your initial network list. Make a note to add them now. You may receive information about the sector that indicates certain employers might have greater need for your services than others, or suggests there are others you should avoid. This is all information that adds depth to your research.

Your aim should be to come away from every meeting with a significant amount of new information and at least two new names to contact.

An ideal situation would be where your contact has suggested a couple of their own contacts who might possibly be able to help you. However, you don't know these people at all. Ideally, you want your contact to phone these people up and ask them if they would mind having a chat with you – preferably a brief meeting. Having someone open the first door to a new contact greatly increases your chances that they will be willing to help, or simply that you will be able to get hold of them at all.

If you ask someone to make a call on your behalf, be prepared to follow the request up. Busy people may intend to do it, but may forget in the hubbub of their daily lives. Suggest calling them in ten days or so to see whether they managed to get hold of Bob or Sally. If they didn't, politely ask again whether they would mind and say you will call again in a week.

The ultimate aim of all this networking is to generate ideas for making speculative approaches to potential employers. We look at this particular job-hunting tactic more closely in Chapter 12.

Portfolio careers

Some people who are natural networkers could be well suited to developing a portfolio career. This approach to career development is likely to become steadily more common in a working world where jobs for life are increasingly rare.

A portfolio career simply brings together a number of different activities and sources of remuneration. Here are a number of examples:

- At a senior level, you might be a non-executive director on a couple of company boards.
- You might, through your business contacts, know of people willing to pay for your advice on an occasional basis – in other words, you offer yourself as a form of independent consultant.
- Do you have a talent for written communication? You might start writing articles for your particular professional association or trade press.
- You could offer training sessions for local organizations in your area of expertise.
- If you have the gift of the gab, could you offer your services as a conference or after dinner speaker?
- You combine a number of part-time jobs – for example, acting as part-time accountant for several small businesses who can't afford a full-time person of their own.

The more people you know, the more sources of different lines of work you have at your fingertips.

Clearly this approach will not suit everyone. Some people will prefer being part of one organization to spreading their talents around many.

In addition, building a portfolio career may well require you to become self-employed, which brings its own issues and you will certainly need to have good business development skills. It takes a certain type of personality to be willing to do without the financial safety net of employment – such as paid holidays and employer pension contributions. There is also the psychological challenge of going it alone, outside the office network.

Nevertheless, there can be compensatory benefits, such as the feeling of increased control over your own destiny, not having a single boss, increased variety in your work and a strong sense of personal achievement.

In practical terms, people most likely to consider a portfolio career are likely to have many years experience under their belts. They might be wanting to step back from having to work 70-hour weeks and see building a portfolio of activities as providing a halfway house between full employment and retirement. Or they might have been made redundant and feel doubtful about whether full-time employment with a single organization is likely to be their best or quickest route back to work.

Whatever your circumstances, consider whether you have the drive to make your portfolio aspirations happen before taking the plunge. You will probably need to work hard initially to establish all the elements you require to generate the quality of work and income level you seek.

Chapter summary: key points

- If you are looking for new challenges, first check whether you really need to move organization.
- Is there potential for promotion within your department?
- If you want a career change, are there opportunities for a sideways move inside your current employer's organization?
- If you need to look elsewhere, think about how your personal contacts may be able to help.
- Networking effectively can enrich your life, as well as your career.

- When trying to make a specific job move, make the most of all your contacts.
- Write a list of absolutely everyone you know, whether or not you think they have any relevant information.
- Starting with those you think most likely to have relevant information, try to arrange a time for a short meeting – perhaps over lunch or coffee.
- Do not ask these people for a job; you are looking for industry information, tips and other useful contacts.
- Try to leave each meeting with at least two new names you can contact.
- All this information from your network may indicate likely potential employers you can target with a speculative letter asking about job openings.
- Portfolio careers may suit effective networkers. It might be worth thinking about whether you have skills that can be used in a number of ways to service different organizations.

Chapter 12

Speculative Approaches

S ome job-seekers, particularly senior executives or those over the age of 40, may find few suitable jobs being advertised in the press. Many recruitment consultancies may also have limited opportunities, unless they are operating at the highest executive level, where there are inevitably fewer jobs available.

In such cases, taking direct action in your job search and making speculative approaches to targeted organizations is likely to be a highly productive route to a new job.

Are speculative approaches worth the effort?

Yes, they are! In our survey almost 90 per cent of HR professionals and line managers said they would read a speculative application. The majority of HR professionals also said that speculative applications would always be considered for current vacancies, as did almost a third of line managers.

You stand a reasonable chance of getting a response, too. Well over half of HR professionals said they would always respond to speculative applications. Although just 23 per cent of line managers said they would always reply, another 51 per cent said they would sometimes or occasionally respond. However, you need to bear in mind that these people receive a lot of speculative applications: the majority of HR professionals we surveyed said they received speculative letters on a daily basis, while a third of line managers received them on a weekly basis. So if you don't hear anything, be prepared to follow up your letter with a phone call. Be persistent!

Also, even if you are told your details will be kept on file, don't believe it. Less than a third of HR professionals said they would consider speculative applications for forthcoming positions. If there is nothing suitable for you now, but you still want to work for this employer, it is up to you to make contact again at a future date.

In summary, speculative applications are worth making. However, if you want your approach to pay off, you must target the right person and stimulate that person's interest *now*. You must make it absolutely obvious why you are worth contacting and meeting.

Sourcing ideas

If you are to maximize your chances of success from a speculative approach to a potential employer, then you need to choose your targets extremely carefully. The aim of your speculative approach (preferably in the form of a letter) is to achieve an interview where you can talk about how you could add value to the organization.

To have any chance of gaining such an interview, your speculative letter must make clear:

- why your particular skills are relevant;
- how your experience could add value; and
- why you are of interest at this stage of the organization's development.

In general terms, your skills and experience are most likely to be relevant to a business or organization similar to the one in which you now work, or where you most recently worked. Your appeal will be maximized by the in-depth sector knowledge you can share.

In contrast, the further you stray in terms of sector, size and location, the less obvious will it be to the targeted employer that you have something useful to offer. If you are currently working for a small advertising agency in London's Soho, you probably won't get a very positive response if you write to a major international manufacturing conglomerate.

Kickstart Tip

As you identify those employers most likely to be interested in your expertise, you should also be looking for the hook on which to hang your speculative approach; this needs to be something that focuses attention further on your particular skills or that highlights the potential value of your experience.

One of the best ways to do this is to identify some event or strategic development that is leading a period of change in the organization. Effective research, as discussed in Chapter 5, Powerful Preparation, holds the key to targeting appropriate organizations. Some leads may come from your networking activities, as considered in Chapter 11, Making Your Own Opportunities. Overall, your research should take in:

- national newspaper reports;
- trade press articles;
- radio business news;
- Internet-based newsletters;
- annual reports and half-yearly statements; and
- insider tips and gossip from your personal contacts.

What hooks to look for

The type of events that you could look out for, depending on your experience, might include:

- forecast expansion;
- mergers and acquisitions;
- planned restructuring;
- new sales route to market;
- expansion overseas;
- new public sector investment; or
- new IT systems development.

Forecast expansion could be relevant if you are:

- a marketing executive with experience of generating rapid sales growth;
- an HR professional with specialist recruitment and development expertise;
- an advertising executive;
- a finance professional with past experience in a rapidly growing organization, skilled in budgeting, forecasting and/or cash control; or
- anyone who previously worked in an organization undergoing rapid expansion – a production manager, quality controller, distribution specialist and so on.

Mergers and acquisitions could be relevant if you are:

- a senior manager with experience in handling business integrations;
- an IT specialist skilled in systems integration projects;
- an HR professional with expertise in handling contractual issues for incoming employees or integrating two businesses; or
- a financial professional with experience in group financial reporting.

Planned restructuring could be relevant if you are:

- a finance professional with venture capital experience;
- a commercial lawyer; or
- anyone with experience in business restructuring, from an HR, IT or general line manager perspective.

A new sales route to market could be relevant if you are:

- a manager with experience in a home shopping business and this is the new direction your targeted established retailer is now taking; or
- an e-commerce strategist and the traditional retailer is expanding into web-based sales.

Expansion overseas could be relevant if you are:

- experienced in doing business in the targeted overseas markets; or
- a fluent linguist in the relevant languages.

New public sector investment could be relevant for:

- anyone with expertise in the targeted sector or specialism; or
- professionals with managerial expertise in handling such investment – for example, involving financial, personnel or legal issues.

IT systems development could be relevant for:

- IT systems integrators;
- IT project managers; or
- functional managers skilled in using the particular new IT system or software.

These are just samples of the kinds of events and hooks that you could use to shape a speculative approach. The more you get into the habit of keeping an eye open for any such items of relevance to your circumstances, the better for your job search.

Getting through the barriers: who to approach

The general rule is: never, ever write to personnel departments – unless you want a job in personnel. Why is this? Our survey found that HR professionals receive speculative letters on a daily basis. Doesn't that mean it is the right thing to do?

No, it does not. The fact that HR departments receive so many letters means that your letter will be just one more item in the in-tray. Yes, your letter may get read, and yes, you may get a response acknowledging your letter, but this doesn't mean you will get the job you want.

Kickstart Tip

Personnel managers can be defined as part of the group of people within the organization who can say 'no' rather than 'yes' to your speculative approach. They will tend to look at their files to see if there are any relevant vacancies at that moment; if there aren't – and the probability is that there won't be – that's the end of your application.

So should you target the top people in the organization, such as the chairman or chief executive? Definitely not. Unless you are trying to get a role as a non-executive chairman, this will also most likely turn out to be a waste of your letter-writing skills. The chairman and chief executive operate at such a high level they probably won't be aware that there is an urgent need for an IT systems integrator in the newly acquired subsidiary.

The golden rule when making speculative approaches is as follows:

● target the person who would be your direct boss.

This is the person who will appreciate whether your skills can be of use, and whether there is now a business need for your expertise, as opposed to an opening available. This is the person who will recognize the *relevance* of your skills because of the situation the organization is currently in, or the events currently taking place. This person will then be focused on the question of '*How can I use her?*' rather than 'Have I got a vacancy?'. This person will be looking for reasons *to employ* you, whereas HR managers will be looking for reasons *not to employ* you.

Whoever you contact, be as precise as possible and make your sale pitch as clear as possible – setting out exactly why you are of interest to them.

Kickstart Tip

So, if you are looking for a position as a financial analyst, write to the finance controller. If you want to get involved in systems integration, contact the IT manager. As a general rule, by targeting relevant senior and middle managers, rather than board-level directors, you stand a better chance of a positive response. That said, if you want a directorship, target the managing director.

Targeting names, not job titles

Once you know who you need to target in terms of job title, you need to find out their name. You should never write to a job title because job titles can't write back and your letter could be redirected to anybody the secretary thinks is appropriate.

If you are targeting a director in a plc, the person's name can easily be found in the annual report and accounts or often from the company's website. If you are using the report and accounts for your source, you might want to double-check that this is still the right person by making a simple call to the company's head office. The main receptionist or switchboard operator should be able to tell you straight away whether Joe Brown is still the finance director.

If you are targeting someone below director level, or someone in a private company, you may need to put in a little more effort to find out the name behind the job role. Again you will need to phone the company and ask for the name of the financial planning manager, for example. You may be asked by reception the reason why you are calling, in which case you can say you are a private individual writing in connection with an employment query; just try to make sure your call is not redirected through to the HR department.

Kickstart Tip

If reception or switchboard tell you the name of the person you want, you should take the opportunity of double-checking its spelling and the address where this person is located, since this may not be at head office.

You might find that you are put through to the targeted individual's PA or secretary, in which case you can double-check this information with them.

Armed with this knowledge, you can at least be reassured that your letter will be heading for the most appropriate person in the organization. To maximize your letter's chances of hitting the target, you might want to mark the envelope 'Personal and Private' rather than 'Private and Confidential'. The more senior your targeted recipient, the more likely that your letter will be opened by a PA or receptionist. If that happens, your letter could still get siphoned off to HR without your target reading it. However, by marking it out as personal correspondence, with luck it will reach the right desk.

Remember that effort is only worth putting in if it is effort targeted in sensible directions. There is no point at all in sending off 200 letters to personnel departments or unknown directors in randomly selected well-known businesses.

It is far better to spend that time identifying 20 key individuals in organizations where there is a clear possibility that you have something to offer them. If you can't explain why you could be useful to the targeted individual at that particular time, then there's no hope at all that the person reading your letter will see any reason to offer you a job.

How to make the approach

We have focused on using a traditional letter format as this is still the best way of getting your message across. A telephone call can easily be intercepted, is likely to be rushed and makes it harder for you to control your message.

An email might be appropriate in some situations, but you run the risk that your email will be assumed to be junk mail and overlooked. Again, many busy managers get their PAs or secretaries to open their emails and deal with them as necessary. So your message could easily be intercepted. Another downside of using emails is that they are easily forgotten once they disappear off the PC screen and become buried among a mass of other emails. A traditional letter is at least in hard-copy form and therefore potentially harder to ignore.

Personal and Private

Mr John Lydiatt
Retail Operations Director
Lexon Retail

Dear Mr Lydiatt

I was interested to read in the business press that Lexon is moving into the area of home shopping. I understand that Lexon Direct is to be launched in the next few months.

You will see from my enclosed CV that I am currently the Planning and Logistics Manager at Webshop.com and was previously Retail Planning Manager at Nexus, the home shopping catalogue. In almost ten years working in retail I have gained a broad range of experience encompassing buying, merchandising and retail operations. More recently I have been directly responsible for establishing a highly successful retail distribution network.

I believe that I can offer directly relevant experience and make a significant contribution to the successful launch of Lexon Direct. I would welcome the opportunity to meet you to discuss how my experience can benefit your company and will call you next week to consider the potential for taking this idea further in person.

Yours sincerely

Mark Long

Mark Long

Figure 12.1 An example speculative letter

Making friends with receptionists and PAs

When you are making a speculative approach to an organization, bear in mind that PAs and secretaries can be a help or a hindrance in assisting your speculative application. They can be a source of information, or they can intercept your speculative letter and divert it elsewhere.

Potential information they can give might include:

- basic information on your targeted individual – such as full name and title;
- brief career history of the targeted individual – e.g. how long they have been in their current role;
- whether there are any obvious current vacancies; and
- how many people work in the department.

How much of this you can find out may depend on how busy the individual is when you call, whether they are in a chatty mood, the cultural climate in the department (e.g. wary of strange enquiries or receptive) and how long they have themselves worked there.

Always be polite and understanding if the PA or secretary is unwilling to discuss any details. You don't want them to take against you and sabotage your letter if they spot it arriving in the post a few days later. On the other hand, if you can get them onside, many PAs and secretaries have persuasive powers over their bosses. If they point out your letter when it comes in, that again increases the chances that it will at least be read, and by your intended recipient.

Chapter summary: key points

- Making speculative approaches to employers can be an effective way to find a new or a dream job.
- Use all available sources of information – newspapers, broadcast news and insider tips – for identifying employers that might have a need for your services.
- Identify for yourself why your skills might be relevant to this employer at this time – this is the hook on which to hang your speculative approach.
- Write a letter that highlights why your skills and experience are relevant and valuable to the employer at this time.

- Avoid HR.
- Target your letter at the individual likely to be your direct boss if your approach is successful.
- Write to this person by name; don't just address your letter to a job title.
- Mark your letter 'Personal and Private'.
- Make friends with receptionists and PAs to maximize the chances of your letter being read by the targeted individual.
- Fewer, highly targeted letters are much more likely to succeed than hundreds of unfocused approaches with no hook.

Part III

From Close Encounters to Closing the Deal

Chapter 13

Interview Savvy

nterviews terrify people – understandably. You are going to face a series of questions from people you don't know in an unfamiliar environment. The interviewer will be trying to identify any weaknesses in your skills and flaws in your character.

Of course, that's just one view.

From another perspective, the interview gives you the opportunity to demonstrate your skills, personality and suitability for the job on offer. Your CV, application form or speculative approach created the opening; the interview provides you with the forum to complete your marketing pitch. Obtaining an interview is a great step forwards towards winning your dream job.

The interviewer's expectations

Before the interview, give a little thought to the interviewer's expectations. Then you can try to meet them more effectively. Interviewers believe that:

- **Candidates need to talk**

  Interviewers have a number of fears, above all silence. The monosyllabic candidate is the interviewer's classic nightmare, because how do you assess someone who doesn't talk? On the other hand, don't go to the opposite extreme and talk for the sake of it; try to offer informative answers that address the topic in question, without digressing into irrelevant areas. The interviewer can always prompt you for more information if necessary. The interviewer is the person theoretically in control of the encounter and you shouldn't try to take that control away.

- **Candidates need to sell themselves**

  Not everyone is good at blowing their own horn. However, you do need to do this in an interview. You need to create in the interviewer's mind the impression that you are the right person for the job. To do this, you have to sell your attributes. Get your message across by giving examples of how your attributes have benefited previous employers. Refer to appraisals or referrals as supporting evidence.

- **Candidates should give opinions**

  It's easy to think of an interview as some kind of a test – a verbal rather than a written one. This tends to focus the attention on providing the right answers or on having the right facts ready. However, interviewers are interested in your opinions and attitudes as well as whether you have the appropriate level of factual or technical knowledge. You need to be able to venture an opinion on any issue thrown at you, and to justify why you feel that way. There may not be an actual right or wrong answer, but you will need to take a stand and explain it.

- **Candidates should take responsibility for establishing rapport**

  This may come as a surprise, but interviewers don't think they should necessarily have to worry about putting you at your ease or finding some initial common ground.

Kickstart Tip

You are the person who needs to take responsibility for establishing rapport with the interviewer.

This is an extremely important element of mastering the interview process, and one considered in more depth below.

Preliminaries

Don't assume that your interviewer will be confident, assured and articulate. They may well be nervous, awkward and scared of silences. While recruitment consultants will be professional interviewers, most line managers within organizations receive no training at all in how to conduct an interview. Try to think about how you can put your interviewer at ease; this tactic not only helps distract you from your own nerves, but also helps to start the interview off on a more relaxed note.

Rapport

Establishing rapport immediately is important for creating a positive atmosphere at the start of the interview; if you can make those first minutes work for you, that positive momentum can carry you forward through the session. The Native Americans have a phrase for rapport that translates roughly as 'Can you wear my moccasins?'. You want to indicate that you can.

First impressions

Evidence shows that first impressions really do count in terms of interview success. Subconsciously, or consciously, the interviewer will be making judgements about you right from the first handshake.

Interviewers filter what they hear based on their first impressions. Your clothes, general appearance, handshake, smile, level of eye contact and small talk are all processed. If in those first seconds of meeting you make a positive impression, the interviewer will make a snap decision that you seem a good sort of person. From that point on, the interviewer will be scanning what you say for confirmation of that assessment, registering the positive elements of your replies more strongly than any negatives.

On the other hand, if you create an initially bad impression, the interviewer will be on the lookout for evidence that confirms their first suspicions – that you aren't the kind of person who would be right for the job.

The art of small talk

The majority of candidates at the start of an interview talk about topics such as their journey or the weather. It's safe material, but doesn't help you to stand out or to catch the interviewer's attention. If you are the fifth person to talk about the jam on the M25 you shouldn't be surprised if your interviewer starts to yawn – inwardly at least.

A more stimulating subject for this preliminary small talk might be some item on the morning's news, perhaps a sports result. You aren't trying to be controversial, just to spark some area of common interest for that first interchange.

Kickstart Tip

Candidates who prepare really well might know some snippet of information about the interviewer. If you have been using a recruitment agency, the consultant may be able to brief you a little on the interviewer's likes, dislikes or interests.

Otherwise, you may have to phone the interviewer's PA. Your excuse might be to ask for some extra information about the organization – such as a brochure or a map of its location. The PA seems friendly and you say, conversationally, 'I haven't met John Roberts [the interviewer] before. Can you tell me anything about him, how long he has been with the organization and what he's like at 8.30 in the morning? That's when I've got my interview.' Make your queries light and unpushy, and the PA will probably be quite happy to give you a quick character sketch. If she tells you some nugget such as, 'Well, Mr Roberts has just become a dad so maybe he'll be a bit tired!' you have an immediate ice-breaker you can use at the start of your interview.

This type of small talk can be put to good use when, for example, the interviewer comes to meet you at reception to take you to the interview room. It can seem a long ride in the lift if you can't think of anything to chat about.

If the interviewer's PA comes to collect you, this again gives you the perfect opportunity to find out some personal snippets of information you can use when you are finally introduced to your interviewer. Don't be afraid to ask. How many people have been seen already that day? Is the interviewer in for a long day? How long have they been with the organization? Are they a nice boss?

The interview masterclass

To become a master of interview technique – and this is a technique that can be learnt and practised – you need to master the 4Ps:

- Preparation
- Presentation
- Personality
- Positive attitude.

Preparation

You must be well-prepared for your interview so that you demonstrate:

- knowledge of the organization's products and services;
- an understanding of market dynamics and competitors;

- appreciation of the value of your functional role;
- a sense of the broader business or organizational perspective; and
- intelligence in the questions you ask the interviewer.

Your preparation process should include:

- reviewing your CV or application form;
- practising likely interview questions; and
- checking the time and location of the interview.

You can never be too well-prepared for an interview. You are aiming to demonstrate your suitability for the job vacancy. If you haven't researched the organization thoroughly, how can you hope to show your suitability?

- **Products and services**

  Our survey respondents rated researching the employer's products and services as the most important preparation an interview candidate can do. The interviewer will expect you to have an understanding both of the environment in which the organization operates, and the specific focus of the organization within it – its own particular mission and strategy.

- **Market dynamics and competitors**

  Having a broad industry knowledge was also seen as particularly important by our survey respondents. You need to understand the competitive stresses in the sector, the positioning of competitors and the opportunities open to your chosen organization. This means you need to have watched the press for any relevant news stories, and to have read the corporate brochures and other public information such as the annual report and accounts.

- **The value of your role**

  You clearly need to demonstrate your skills in relation to your particular target job role. How could you add value to the organization in this particular role?

  If you are applying for an accounting position, you might need to be able to discuss a recent change in accounting practice; if you are an IT guru, you might be asked to venture an opinion on recent Internet security breaches.

- **Broad business or organizational perspective**
  Being able to demonstrate a broad business perspective is becoming particularly important, no matter what particular role you are applying for. Finance professionals need to show they understand the importance of branding and marketing activity; marketing professionals need to show they understand the importance of maintaining stock market value; human resource people need to indicate they understand the importance of staff policy for creating a favourable public reputation; and so on. You need to be able to talk the big picture.

- **Intelligent questions**
  Doing a bit of cramming gives you the reassurance that you should be able to cope with the questions the interviewer throws at you. It also helps you come up with questions that you can thrown back at the interviewer. One highly successful female job-hunter, who has always been offered a job after an interview, does this to great effect. An accountant in industry, she comes up with one or two difficult or interesting questions for her interviewer based on her review of the published accounts. She picks some small item, perhaps relating to the accounting treatment of an acquisition, and queries the rationale behind it. This tactic not only allows her to demonstrate her technical knowledge, but also shows how thoroughly she has researched the target company.

- **Review your CV or application form**
  Your pre-interview preparation needs to include a review of the CV or application form you sent in for this particular job. This is particularly important if you are applying for several different jobs so that there are several versions of your CV in circulation. Try to identify any areas that the interviews might want to focus on, perhaps your claim about a recent systems implementation or your successful sales drive.

- **Practising likely questions**
  Make notes of any likely questions you expect to be asked, based on your knowledge of the marketplace, the organization, your job specialism and your CV. Then start practising answers. In the next chapter we consider in detail potential answers to the most frequently asked interview questions.

- **Interview time and place**

  One piece of mundane but essential preparation involves making sure you know exactly where you have got to be and when. You must be on time. Remember to take a map if you have any doubts about getting lost. Even better, visit the location of the interview office beforehand so you know how long it takes to get there. Another useful tactic is to identify a nearby coffee bar where you can plan to arrive early, have a drink, use the loos, wash your hands and compose yourself before the final advance to the organization's premises.

Presentation

Your clothes and general self-presentation may be more important than you think for determining interview success or failure. Research suggests that how you dress and how you speak (the quality of your voice and the correct use of grammar) can have a greater impact on forming the interviewer's opinion than the actual content of what you say. While you can't necessarily expect to change the way you speak overnight, you can make an effort to avoid jargon, slang and swearing. You can also spend a little time thinking about the clothes you wear for your interview.

To present yourself in the best light through your clothes you should:

- dress formally;
- select darker colours;
- look up-to-date;
- avoid white socks and excessive jewellery (if you are male);
- avoid cardigans but do dab on a little make-up (if you are female); and
- make sure your baggage looks the part.

Some of this may sound petty. It isn't!

Just imagine if two equivalent candidates are interviewed. Both have the paper qualifications and the interpersonal skills. There's nothing to choose between them, except that one looks the part – wearing a serious suit – and the other doesn't. Who do you think gets the job? Don't put yourself at a disadvantage by not bothering to present yourself properly.

- **Dress formally**

  Don't think of the interview as an ordinary meeting; it is a formal occasion. Therefore, be warned. Even if you know that the company to which you are applying operates a casual dress code, don't turn up in chinos and an open-neck shirt. You haven't been invited to join the organization yet and should dress as you would if you were going to an important business occasion where your image was a vital contributory element towards sealing a deal – this is actually exactly what you are doing.

  Although women generally enjoy more flexibility in the clothes they can wear in the workplace, a suit is again the recommended clothing for maximising professional impact at an interview.

- **Pick darker colours**

  Given the importance of formality, note that dark colours convey a more professional image than light ones. Even on a hot summer's day, you are more likely to create a positive impact by wearing a dark blue suit; leave the beige or fawn number behind in the wardrobe.

  There may, of course, be some cultural variations across countries and continents. In the UK and the United States a business suit is the only wise option for interview dress; however, in continental Europe, particularly Italy and Belgium, a sports jacket and trousers may be appropriate. If in doubt, choose the more formal of any option.

- **Look up-to-date**

  Whatever you choose to wear, make sure it looks up-to-date. You may have a favourite interview suit, but if it is now ten years old and looks it, you should invest in a new one.

- **Male issues**

  Men should avoid wearing white socks. Grey shoes don't usually look too impressive either. Try not to display too much jewellery or be drenched in aftershave.

- **Female issues**

  There is no such thing as the power cardie! Leave your cardigans behind. It is also worth noting that research shows that women who wear some make-up in general tend to be more successful than women who wear none. However, if you go over the top and slap on too much, that can create a worse impression than wearing no make-up at all.

- **Professional baggage only**

  In terms of the baggage you turn up with, try to keep it to a minimum. On no account arrive for the interview carrying plastic bags. If you do need to bring some kind of bag, make sure it's a briefcase. Nor do you want to insist on pulling out piles of supporting documents that demonstrate how great your work is. If evidence of this kind is appropriate to the job role, wait to be invited to produce it. Let the interviewer know you have the documents with you, but don't force them to have a look.

- **Every detail counts**

  Mary Spillane of Imageworks, a renowned image consultant and author of Branding Yourself, offers the following advice:

  > Pay attention to all the details. We communicate with our hands, so if your hands are in rough shape, we notice. What about the quality of the pen you carry? Be aware of the state of your shoes; and women should pay attention to the quality of the tights they wear. As for grooming, just being clean is not enough. If you have blotches that are distracting, get them sorted out so they are not an issue. Concealer works wonders for men in their late 30s and beyond who get circles under their eye. They should get the women in their lives to show them a few tricks.

Personality

You have been invited to an interview because on paper you appear to be suitable for the vacancy. At the interview, while double-checking that suitability, the interviewer will also be trying to get a sense of your personality.

As a candidate, you don't want to hide your own personality – you should be yourself – but you do want to emphasize your most positive and professional aspects. Therefore, there are a number of things you can do to create a favourable impression of your personality. These include:

- maintaining eye contact;
- smiling;
- monitoring the interviewer's body language;
- responding to the interviewer's personal style; and
- shaking hands firmly.

The more naturally you can do these things, the more relaxed, confident and professional you will appear.

- **Maintain eye contact**
  Some people find maintaining eye contact particularly difficult when they are nervous. Unfortunately, your chances of success at the interview will be significantly reduced if you insist on staring at your shoes, the desk or out of the window, rather than at your interviewer. You shouldn't try to stare the interviewer down, but if you never meet their eyes you will appear shifty, nervous or bored.

Kickstart Tip

The interviewer's eyes are themselves a useful source of information about how the interview is going – whether you are talking too much, too little, and so on. The phrase 'eyes glazing over' has real meaning!

If you really can't maintain eye-to-eye contact for extended periods, try focusing on the interviewer's mouth as a near alternative. Be aware that you may be interviewed by more than one person, particularly if you are applying for a public sector job, as we discussed in Chapter 3, Planning an Effective Job Search. Although you should direct your opening words in response to a question to the individual who asked it, try also to include all the members of the panel in the discussion by engaging in eye contact with them as well.

- **Smile**
  Nothing beats a smile for creating a positive atmosphere. If you appear someone with a positive outlook on life, so much the better. Sharing a little humour can also work to your advantage, though this should be natural and result from the natural flow of the conversation. You don't want to start telling jokes (unless your interviewer asks you to, which is unlikely).

- **Monitor the interviewer's body language**
  Monitoring the overall body language of the interviewer can help tell you something about the person facing you and their reaction to you. It may be that the interviewer isn't actually very good at maintaining eye contact. Perhaps they are inexperienced at the interview game and therefore extremely nervous. In this case, you can help

things along by working hard to establish rapport. Or the lack of eye contact may mean you are losing the interviewer's interest, in which case you might want to cut your reply short and give the interviewer a chance to respond, or perhaps throw in a question yourself.

- **Respond to the interviewer's personal style**
As the interview progresses you can adjust your style to that of the interviewer. For example, say you are a natural extrovert – with a loud voice and lots of opinions. You meet your interviewer who is a quiet, reserved personality. If you realize that you are personality-type opposites, you might want to tone down your natural exuberance to try to match your interviewer more closely. This doesn't mean lying about the kind of person you are; you are simply responding to your environment and doing all you can to get on with the person interviewing you.

- **Shake hands firmly**
Finally, you can create the impression that you are a confident personality by offering a firm (though not knuckle-breaking) handshake on arrival and departure. If you have a tendency for sweaty hands, particularly when under stress, try to arrive early so you can wash them before going in to meet your interviewer

Positive attitude

Our research asked respondents to rate the importance of a range of factors that might influence their decision about an interviewee. Enthusiasm emerged as the highest-rated factor in influencing the recruiter's decision – mentioned by 81 per cent of our survey respondents.

Positivity is a highly appealing attribute in an interview candidate. To display a positive attitude you should:

- act as if you really want the job;
- not think about whether you do want the job until after the interview;
- remember that enthusiastic, positive candidates receive more job offers; and
- remain positive right to the end.

No matter what happens during the interview, you must keep on giving out positive vibes.

- **Act as if you really want the job**

  Remember: your aim during the interview is not to get the job; it is simply to get the offer of the job. Your presence at the interview doesn't mean you necessarily want this position in the end, but you should act as if you do. You may actually have significant doubts about whether the job is right for you, but you don't give a hint of them.

- **Don't think about whether you do want the job until after the interview**

  When you arrive for your interview you may never have met someone from the organization, and you may not have a real understanding of its culture or what would be required of you. You will gather information on these issues during the interview, but you must not start assessing the job – and the offer – until you can do so calmly at home.

- **Enthusiastic, positive candidates receive more job offers**

  During the interview itself you must be 100 per cent in marketing mode, presenting your best attributes and giving off positive vibes about the organization and the job role.

  Think about this from the interviewer's perspective. This person has got the responsibility of selecting an individual from a list of candidates. Once they have made a decision as to their preferred choice, they want to feel confident that the individual will accept the job. They don't want to waste time, or look foolish to their colleagues, by being rejected.

  So, imagine the decision comes down to two candidates. The first is superbly qualified for the job, has all the right skills and personal attributes. The second is also highly able but perhaps lacks experience in one area. The first candidate should be the first choice, except for the fact that he expressed some hesitancy about why he wanted the job and suggested that he was following up a couple of other options. The second candidate was extremely enthusiastic; she expressed great interest in the department and the interviewer and had an extremely positive outlook, expressing willingness to pick up speed in her area of weakness as fast as possible.

  You, the interviewer, want this position filled fast. You are pretty confident that candidate two will be able to do the job and that she will accept if offered the position. You think candidate one might refuse. What do you do?

  You will almost certainly offer the job to candidate number two.

Kickstart Tip

Evidence shows that, in the final analysis, job offers are often made to the candidate most likely to accept.

- **Remain positive right to the end**

  You need to maintain your positive attitude until you have left the interviewer's premises. If you are walking to the exit making conversation with your interviewer, don't relax too much. If you are asked what you are up to that afternoon and you say you have to go to one of those 'dreadful team meetings', this may jar unfavourably on the interview's ears if you have just been talking about how well you get on with your colleagues and how being a team player is one of your strongest attributes.

Money talk

In Chapter 16, Negotiating the Best Job Offer we look at how to go about getting the best deal in terms of pay and benefits.

Kickstart Tip

It's worth noting that whenever possible you should try to avoid talking during the interview stage about the salary you would want if you were to take the job.

This can require canny tongue work if you are asked directly what you would expect to be paid, so you might want to think about your answer in advance. Try at all times to stress your enthusiasm for the job and its appeal in terms of the challenges, the opportunity and responsibility it would offer you.

If pushed, you might try to avoid giving a direct answer by referring to your current package, while avoiding saying how much higher the job offer would need to go. If your interviewer is tenacious, you could perhaps refer to the job advert or some figure that your recruitment consultant has mentioned to you. You can simply indicate that negotiations around that mark would be suitable, but repeat that the package is not the key issue for you at this stage. You are more interested in the other rewards the job itself has to offer.

Turn-offs

Our survey of HR professionals, line managers and headhunters identified the biggest mistakes candidates can make at the interview stage. These fall into a number of general themes.

General approach to the interview

- making an inadequate contribution to the interview process;
- attempting to run the interview;
- not asking questions;
- not understanding what the job is about; and
- not having done enough research into the job and employer.

Enthusiasm and confidence

- showing a lack of interest or enthusiasm;
- wanting the job at any cost;
- being overconfident or overselling themselves;
- arrogance;
- lack of confidence and shyness;
- failing to demonstrate achievements;
- being too casual or flippant; and
- appearing lazy or dull.

Quality of answers

- lying or trying to bluff;
- waffling, rambling and generally talking too much;
- giving monosyllabic answers;
- not listening to the question;
- not answering the question asked;
- giving inarticulate answers; and
- giving answers they think the interviewer wants to hear, rather than expressing their own opinions.

Self-presentation

- poor body language, failure to make eye contact;
- not smiling;
- untidy or inappropriate appearance;
- using inappropriate language (e.g. racist, sexist or overfriendly);
- appearing to have a poor attitude to work; and
- appearing to get stressed under pressure.

Basic courtesy

- arriving late;
- receiving calls on mobile phones;
- rudeness; and
- being aggressive.

Other flaws

- showing too much interest in the money or talking about the salary at too early a stage;
- focusing on career prospects rather than the job in question;
- running down the present employer or job held; and
- asking questions focused on hours, holidays or personal needs.

Some of these survey responses indicate the fine line that candidates need to tread. For example, interviewers expect you to make a contribution to making the interview swing along, but they don't want you to try to dominate it. Similarly, they don't like overconfidence, but nor does a lack of confidence impress them. They want you to be able to demonstrate your achievements, but find overselling a turn-off.

Your best approach is to apply common sense, avoid extremes and try to respond to any signals the interviewer gives you.

General rudeness

On the subject of rudeness, don't assume you only have to be nice to the interviewer and can forget about the impression you make on the other people you meet before or after your interview. You can lose a job by being rude or arrogant when speaking to a receptionist or PA. Imagine you are the interviewer, escorting an interview candidate to the door. You shake the interviewee's hand and turn away smiling. The candidate has done well and is your preferred choice so far. Then the receptionist grimaces. 'I hope you're not going to give him a job,' she says.

You are shocked. 'Why's that?'

The receptionist tells you how rude the candidate was about the lack of available car parking spaces and then having to wait in reception for 20 minutes. As an interviewer, your positive impression is immediately punctured and you may start wondering whether the individual was just putting on an act.

Recruiters' top tips for interview success

Our research asked the HR professionals, line managers and headhunters for their best advice for someone preparing for an interview. Their tips underline the advice given earlier in this chapter and provide a helpful summary.

Their key tips are:

- Conduct thorough research into the company or employer so you appear well-prepared.
- Role-play or practise before the interview.
- Try to smile, be calm, relaxed and be yourself.
- Be honest and avoid pretence.
- Have some relevant prepared questions you can ask.
- Understand the job.
- Be clear about your reasons for applying.
- Know what it is you can bring to the job.
- Don't be afraid to talk about yourself and to sell yourself.
- Be enthusiastic.
- Show an interest in the business.
- Be positive.
- Be friendly.
- Be confident in your abilities.
- Be prepared to talk about your achievements.

- Dress smartly and look the part.
- Listen carefully to each question.
- Answer the questions and be prepared to expand on your answers.
- Be punctual.

None of this is rocket science, but it's surprising how often people make basic mistakes. If you can successfully apply this advice in your interviews, you will be showing yourself in the best possible light and stealing a march on less savvy applicants.

If you know you have done your best, all you can do then is wait for the recruiter to let you know the outcome.

Although some applicants try to add a final boost to their sales pitch by writing in after the interview stressing their continued interest in the post, this is probably a waste of time. In our survey, over three-quarters of recruiters said that sending in a follow-up letter after the interview was not useful.

Chapter summary: key points

- Check the time and location of the interview.
- Review your CV or application form beforehand.
- Practise likely interview questions.
- First impressions count! Smile and shake hands firmly.
- Take responsibility for building rapport with the interviewer.
- Think up some topics for opening small talk.
- During your interview, be prepared to talk, sell yourself and give opinions.
- Preparation is essential for interview success.
- You must show knowledge of the organization's products or services.
- Display an understanding of market dynamics and competitors.
- Demonstrate the value of your functional role.
- Indicate you have a broader business or organizational perspective.
- Prepare questions for the interviewer based on your knowledge of the organization.
- How you present yourself can be more important than what you say.
- You should dress formally, select darker colours, look up-to-date and avoid fashion faux pas.
- Make sure your baggage looks professional.

- Maintain eye contact, smile, monitor the interviewer's body language and respond to the interviewer's personal style.
- A positive attitude and enthusiasm are essential.
- Act as if you really want the job.
- Avoid talking about the salary you would require.

Chapter 14

Tackling Frequently Asked Interview Questions

P reparation is the key to job-hunting success. This is nowhere more true than in the context of the interview.

If an interview is an exam, then it's an exam where you are pretty much given the exam questions the night before. What do we mean by this? Well, the reality is that interviewers are notoriously uninventive – most of them ask fairly typical questions. They want to know about your past work experience and your personal qualities. To do this, the precise wording of the questions they ask may differ slightly, but the themes and the required content of the answers will be fairly standard.

Kickstart Tip

You are more likely to perform well at interview if you have prepared answers to the most common questions. In fact, preparing answers to interview questions is essential if you are to maximize your impact.

Interview styles

Although the majority of human resource professionals will have undergone a degree of training in interview techniques, the same cannot be said of line managers, of whom only a small minority will have received any interview training at all. Some will even talk for more time than they will listen, so as an interviewee, you need to make your answers count.

However, those recruiters with some understanding of effective interviewing will try to apply a number of techniques:

- avoiding closed (yes/no) questions;
- avoiding leading questions (which give you an idea of the desired answer); and
- asking competency-based or behavioural questions.

Interviewers vary in the use they make of theoretical or hypothetical questions such as 'What would you do if . . . ?' Although such questions don't give the interviewer any information about how you would really act in such a situation, they can give an insight into your thought processes. If given an unfamiliar scenario, can you structure a logical or creative response? Theoretical or hypothetical questions are therefore most likely to be used in interviews for particularly creative or analytical jobs. If this is you, be prepared to think on your feet.

Competency-based interviewing

Competency-based interviewing (CBI), also referred to as behavioural event interviewing (BEI), is based on the premise that the past is a good predictor of the future or, in other words, leopards don't change their spots.

The technique aims to give the interviewer an idea of how the candidate has performed in real life. It looks for evidence of skills, experience and behaviour that can be seen as indicative of future job performance, development potential and fit with organizational culture.

The key to impressing an experienced interviewer using the CBI technique is therefore to have a wealth of examples at your mental fingertips. You want a range of past challenges, problems, successes and learning experiences that you can recount concisely, that show you in a positive light.

However, whether or not your interviewer is using the CBI approach, providing answers that draw on your experiences is still the best method of stressing your suitability for the role in question.

Answer preparation

Allow enough preparation time for identifying likely questions you might be asked and then for going through suitable answers. You might want to do this in several stages, first jotting down notes of key points you want to get across, including examples that illustrate your answers. You could then practise turning those notes into spoken language and finally, practise with the help of someone you know well – a friend, partner, husband or wife. Ask them to play the interviewer and have a dummy run, checking you don't chatter on too much and that your replies are sufficiently informative.

When preparing possible answers, bear in mind the following guidelines:

- **Use real, working life examples wherever possible**

  You don't want to make statements such as 'I'm good at managing staff'. You need to use examples that demonstrate *how* you are good at managing staff. The interviewer is far more likely to believe you and to remember your qualities.

- **Draw on job appraisals and reviews for blowing your trumpet**

  Some nationalities are happier than others about hearing people sing their own praises. In Britain, for example, you may come over as too cocky when you are trying to sell yourself. One technique that can soften the style of delivery, but provide persuasive evidence of your abilities, is to refer to situations where other people have praised your abilities or actions, such as formal appraisals and job reviews.

- **Try to demonstrate so-called softer management skills**

  Communication ability, team-working and other soft skills are increasingly important in the world of open-plan offices and flattened hierarchies. Where possible, combine hard evidence of your success (e.g. improved revenues, reduced costs) with softer issues (e.g. improved staff morale).

- **Try to illustrate innovative or new ideas you have introduced**

  Employers find innovation a highly appealing concept, but make sure you can talk about *how* you took your ideas from drawing board to reality.

- **Be concise**

  Practise delivering answers that last no more than two or three minutes. You don't want to dominate the interview or bore your interviewer.

Predicting likely questions

There may be some questions related to your specific circumstances. ('Why did you leave your degree course halfway through?')

These you need to identify for yourself and have some convincing answers ready. Look through your CV with the eyes of an interviewer and imagine what you would want to ask. If you have done anything odd or unusual, if your career takes an unexpected twist or turn, be ready to explain why this is so in a logical manner.

However, most people can expect to be asked a fairly standard range of questions. In researching this book, our questionnaire asked for examples of the questions recruiters felt were most revealing about candidates. Strong common themes emerged. These included:

Challenges and achievements

- What is the most difficult experience you have had to deal with?
- What is the most challenging issue you have encountered?
- What is your greatest career achievement?
- What improvements did you initiate in your last job?

The job applied for/the company applied to

- Why have you applied for this position?
- Why do you think you are suited to this position?
- What skills and experience can you bring to this position?
- What are you looking for from this position?
- What do you know about this company/organization?
- Want do you see as the key issues affecting this industry or sector?

Current role

- Why are you leaving your current job?
- What do you like about your current job?
- What do you dislike about your current job?
- How would you describe your current role?

Your profession

- Why did you choose this profession? (Law, accountancy, marketing etc.)
- What is your view on this issue? (Related to a current technical debate.)

Personal strengths and weaknesses

- What are your main strengths?
- Why should this company employ you (ahead of other applicants)?
- What are your weaknesses?
- What was your biggest mistake?

Management qualities

- Give me an example of your leadership ability.
- How do you handle responsibility?
- How would you deal with a problem such as . . .?
- How have you dealt with a difficult management situation?
- How do you deal with difficult people?
- How do you handle difficult clients?
- How do you handle change?
- What motivates you?
- How would you describe your work ethic?
- How would your work colleagues describe you?
- What makes you a good team player?
- How would your boss describe you?
- Describe your ideal boss.
- Tell me about yourself.
- What would you most like to change about yourself or your skills?
- What makes you laugh?
- What personal interests do you have outside work?

Aspirations

- Describe your ideal job or working environment.
- What is most important to you in your job?
- Where will you be in five to ten years' time?
- What are your future plans?
- What were your objectives five years ago, and have you achieved them?
- What was your biggest disappointment?
- Talk me through your career to date.

Suggested answers

We have not attempted to provide answers to all these questions since many are simply variations of others. However, we have selected some for detailed examination. We consider what the interviewer is trying to get at by asking the question, and how you should structure your response. In some cases we include a fictional answer as an example of how you could phrase your own reply.

You should review all the questions above and practise structuring your own answers.

Remember to think about the interviewer's objectives and how you can meet those needs while showing yourself to your best advantage.

What is the most difficult experience you have had to deal with?

The interviewer's aim

Questions that ask about your most difficult experience, biggest problem or greatest challenge are trying to uncover how you deal with problems and challenges. Are you someone who can find a solution or do you panic? Do you learn from tough experiences?

How to reply

In general, you want to identify an experience related to the workplace. (If in doubt, clarify with the interviewer whether a general life experience is of interest.) You also want to choose an experience with a positive outcome, which you learnt from.

You could structure your reply so that you initially flag up what you learnt, and then recount the story that leads to that conclusion.

Sample answer

My most difficult work experience was perhaps in my first sales job. At the time it was really tough, but it did have a positive outcome in that I became determined to develop my presentational skills.

This particular experience happened about ten years ago when I was working as a junior sales manager for Hypergrowth plc. We had been invited to pitch for a lucrative contract to supply a major UK company and I was called in to help prepare the bid documents and material for the presentation. My boss was a real character and a great salesman, so he was going to do all the talking. He didn't like using notes, but he wanted me to help prepare some supporting slides. We were booked to see the client on a Thursday morning. On the Wednesday afternoon my boss was suddenly taken ill with chest pains. He told me to go ahead and give the presentation in his place. I was terrified. I spent most of Wednesday evening practising but I hadn't had any training in this area.

Thursday came and I went off to give the presentation, taking my own assistant with me. I was extremely nervous and in the first five minutes I confused a couple of the slides, which made me look like I didn't know what I was talking about. I did really; I was just suffering from nerves and inexperience. In the end I got into my stride, but we didn't win the contract.

After that, I signed myself up straightaway for presentational training and insisted that I take an active part in the next presentation my boss gave. After a little more experience I found I began to enjoy it. Six months later I gave another solo pitch and won the deal. I don't think that would have happened if I hadn't had such a shock the first time.

What is your greatest career achievement?

The interviewer's aim

This kind of question is giving you the chance to sell yourself. The interviewer wants to check that you are an achiever and that you believe in yourself.

How to reply

Offer an achievement that has some relevance to the job vacancy, even in general terms. Make it clear why you consider this to be your greatest career achievement. Where possible, refer to an objective assessment of what you did – perhaps a client comment or high praise received in your annual performance review. You don't want to sound as if you are blowing your own trumpet without just cause.

Sample answer

My greatest achievement to date was in opening up the French market for my current organization. The firm had made several unsuccessful attempts in the last few years, and when I took my current role two years ago, this was made a high priority for me.

I realized that part of the problem had been a failure to allocate dedicated sales representatives who could build up long-term relationships with our French customers. Nor had we successfully identified the most appropriate French companies to target as our key customer base; we were too unfocused in our approach. Finally, I didn't think our marketing material appropriately reflected the French market's needs.

I formed a French market taskforce to discuss these ideas and come up with some other suggestions for how we could crack the market, which we then put into practice. That was two years ago and we immediately saw positive results. In the first year we increased turnover generated in France by 100 per cent. This year we achieved a 300 per cent increase. Our European sales director recently asked me to prepare a report for the board explaining how we achieved this result and suggesting how we can roll the approach out across our sales teams in Germany and Spain as well. My recent appraisal commented on the quality of this report and praised me for my success in France. It also credited me with the improved morale among our staff, which I think is actually a by-product of our department's success.

Why do you think you are suited to this position?

The interviewer's aim

This is an open invitation to show that you have thought about the role and that you have confidence in your ability to fill it well. The interviewer wants to identify whether you have relevant experience for the position.

How to reply

The initial job advertisement or the job brief given to the recruitment consultant will include a number of areas of skills and experiences that the employer believes necessary for the role. Your answer should indicate your understanding of these key areas, prioritize them and give examples of how you have obtained the necessary experience and developed the required skills in a similar role. You shouldn't simply state that you have the skills required – give evidence.

Sample answer

I understand that staff management experience is important for this role. In my current position I am responsible for supervising a team of 16 people, six directly. It's a part of my work that I greatly enjoy. Two years ago, when I took on my current role, we had some problems retaining people in the department so I made a point of talking to staff about their key concerns and needs. It seemed that many felt they weren't given enough feedback about their performance or made to feel that the company valued what they did. As a result I liaised with personnel to improve the appraisal forms we were using, to make them more relevant to my team. I also organized a seminar in which we discussed, as a group, how our work contributed to corporate performance and ways in which that could be improved. Our staff turnover has since become one of the lowest in the organization.

Systems implementation experience is also required for this vacancy. As it happens I have just been involved in implementing a multi-currency system across all our locations. I helped to specify the system requirements and plan the roll-out. This was my first experience of a multi-location systems implementation, and it emphasized for me the importance of clear communication and regular, specific progress reports. Although we encountered a few setbacks along the way, we managed to make up time in the later stages and completed the implementation on time.

Finally, I believe that thriving on change is a key requirement for success in this post. I have always sought out roles where there was some element of change in management required. I previously worked for Merger plc when they were applying their acquisitions strategy. The internal organization was in a continual state of flux, which was very exciting. It meant there were lots of opportunities for people willing to take responsibility. For example, I became involved in managing the consolidation of two acquired businesses, which was extremely challenging because we had to cope with running two different reporting systems for almost a year. However, we were successful in achieving 90 per cent of the identified post-merger benefits within the first 18 months after the acquisitions.

What are you looking for from this position?

The interviewer's aim

To see whether your aspirations fit the job description, and how well you understand what the position entails.

How to reply

You are looking only for things that you know the job will give you. Some interviewers will open proceedings by giving you a summary of what the role involves. This is valuable information that you can reword and repeat back when answering questions such as this. For example, say the interviewer has told you that the department needs someone who can analyse the wide range of data that is sent in from overseas locations every month. You can use that information:

> I am looking for the potential to develop my analytical skills further. I was recently praised for my analysis of our UK regional performance, but I am keen to build in an international element to my experience. I believe this role would enable me to enhance my current analytical expertise while broadening my horizons to incorporate multinational issues.

What do you know about this company/organization?

The interviewer's aim

This question is simply designed to check you have done some research.

How to reply

Don't say 'Not a lot' or 'Only what the recruitment consultancy told me'. Your reply should indicate that you have researched the organization and its sector, potentially including references to its recent performance, product or service development, who its competitors are and how they are doing, notable market events and key directors. Refer to your sources, such as news reports, marketing material, the company website and the annual report and accounts.

Your answer should make it clear that your research has reinforced your desire to work for the organization, rather than its competitors. For example:

> I know from your annual report that you are the market leader in rust resistant paint, and increasing your market share in weatherproof varnishes. That struck a chord because it's important to me to work for a company that's leading its field.

Why are you leaving your current job?

The interviewer's aim

To find out whether you are being pushed out or leaving because you are attracted by the pull of better opportunities elsewhere.

How to reply

Never bad-mouth your current employer. Nor should you try to hide something that is likely to come to light at a later date. However, given that most job moves are the result of a push and a pull, you want to emphasize the positive pull of the new job rather than the negative push of your old one. Be prepared for some probing. One wily interviewer's trick was to ask the 'Why are you leaving?' question, listen to the answer, and then fire back, 'OK, so now tell me why you are *really* leaving.'

Sample answer

I have gained a lot of good experience and enjoyed my work thoroughly. However, after three years I feel there are few challenges left. I believe the time is right to broaden my experience, which is why I am attracted to this position. It would enable me to develop my knowledge of the UK marketplace while gaining exposure to US practices.
OR
I wasn't actually planning to leave just yet. I am still gaining useful experience and would happily remain where I am for another year. However, a friend of mine told me about this opportunity and I decided it was too good to miss.
OR

It is public knowledge now that Struggle plc is in some financial difficulty following the recent fall in investor interest in smaller listed companies and so I believe it is in my best interests to look for a role in a larger organization. However, I am not willing to take the first job that comes along. This role appears to offer the potential for me to develop my marketing skills in a thriving environment, while sharing my experience in managing advertising campaigns on a cost-effective budget.

What do you like or dislike about your current job?

The interviewer's aim

As above, the interviewer may think your answer will throw some light on why you want to leave. The interviewer will also be checking that there is consistency between the aspects of your current role that you like and the features of the job on offer.

How to answer

Dwell on positive issues rather than negatives. The aspects you say you like in your current job should be available to you if you are appointed to the role you seek. There's no point saying you love the international travel you now have if the vacancy will require you to spend all your time at head office. Be shrewd! And while it's good to say that you enjoy the companionship of your colleagues, you don't want to give the impression that you just go to work for the gossip and giggles.

In terms of dislikes, try to avoid sounding too vehement about anything. You shouldn't try to hide key issues that the recruiter may subsequently find out about, but you don't want to give the impression that any particular dislike is so strong as to force you to leave your current job. Nor do you want to come over as a whinger; positive personalities are always more attractive.

How would you describe your current role?

The interviewer's aim

To find out more about you, particularly whether you have appropriate experience for the vacant position. The interviewer also wants to discover if you understand how your role interrelates with other functions and contributes to the performance of the organization.

How to reply

Don't try to describe your entire job in great detail. Highlight your key areas of responsibility, preferably ones that are most relevant to the job you are applying for. You shouldn't lie, but you can emphasize some areas of your current activity and underplay others in order to illustrate your suitability.

What are your main strengths?

The interviewer's aim

To find out whether your declared strong points match those required for the job.

How to reply

This question should be answered in a similar way to questions asking about why you think you are suited to the role (see above). Above all, choose strengths that are appropriate to the job you have applied for. Then give succinct examples of where your strengths have proved useful to past employers, or offer objective evidence they exist, referring to appraisals or positive business outcomes.

What are your weaknesses?

The interviewer's aim

This is the kind of question that interviewers like to ask because it can make candidates squirm. At face value, the interviewer wants to know whether you will reveal any flaws which could make you unsuitable for the job. It's also the type of question which brings out the individual's ability to turn a negative into a positive.

How to reply

Questions like this require a politician's answer. You don't want to dwell on negative aspects, but you have to come up with something, since no one really is perfect. One approach is to pick a weakness that might not really be considered a weakness. For example, you could say you perhaps are *too* dedicated to your work and your family sometimes feels the impact, although your office gets the benefit.

A variation on this approach is to acknowledge that there are areas where you have development needs, perhaps in terms of IT training, but that you have tackled such issues successfully in the past. In this way you indicate that you understand the importance of continued self-development and learning and that you are aware of your own potential for positive improvement. You could illustrate this with an example of a past weakness that you identified and subsequently rectified, or even turned into a strength.

Possible past weaknesses could have been:

- nerves when public speaking (now rectified through training and experience);
- IT skills (now a strength as a result of training and on-the-job development);
- being too much of a perfectionist (a bit of an old chestnut, but acceptable – maybe you have since learnt to be more pragmatic about the use of your time);
- presenteeism (staying in the office for long hours because it was expected, rather than productive – perhaps you are now more confident about determining the hours you work); or
- poor delegation skills (you have since learnt that trusting staff to handle important issues brings out the best in them, provided they have appropriate training and support).

Another approach is to pick a weakness that has no repercussions for the job in question. For example, if you are applying for a role that involves no staff management at all and no prospect of it in future, then there shouldn't be a problem if you say one of your weaknesses is that you really don't enjoy managing other people.

The other side of the coin applies: you must never give as a weakness some characteristic that is clearly essential for the job applied for. If you do, your application will move straight to the reject pile.

What was your biggest mistake?

The interviewer's aim

Questions that ask about your biggest mistake, failure or disappointment are trying to find out how you cope with setbacks. Everyone makes mistakes sometimes, but not everyone learns from them. Similarly, everyone has to cope with some disappointments. Are you a tough enough character to bounce back?

How to reply

You want to demonstrate that you are someone who learns from mistakes. If possible, choose an example with some kind of positive outcome.

Sample answer

Three years ago I made a snap decision about how much of a certain product we were going to buy in. Normally I spoke to all the local reps before taking such a step, but on this occasion I was being pressed for a quick order (in return for a discount) and I decided that, as this product in the past had been a hot seller, any decision was better than none. Unfortunately, the supplier was unexpectedly in financial difficulty, which my reps could have told me. We received our delivery but the product didn't sell well because people knew there might be problems with the warranties. That meant we had to come up with some creative marketing techniques to stimulate sales, including offering some discounts ourselves. Fortunately, things turned out OK and we covered our costs in the end, plus a small margin. However, I haven't made the same mistake again. The experience taught me that it is worth taking time – even if you have to stall slightly – to get all key facts or speak to any key people before making such commercial decisions.

How have you dealt with a difficult management situation?

The interviewer's aim

To get a feel for your management style. Are you confrontational or diplomatic? Are you methodical or happy to take rapid decisions? Both approaches could suit different organizations or different positions, depending on particular circumstances at the time.

How to reply

Pick an example which you think relevant to the job vacancy, and one which shows you in a light you consider would be seen as positive by the recruiting organization. Shape your answer so as to briefly explain the situation, why it was difficult, how you went about dealing with it and what the outcome was (expressed in objective or measurable terms). You may not know what style the recruiter is really looking for, so try to be true to yourself when picking your example.

How do you deal with difficult people?

The interviewer's aim

To see how you interact with other people – be they colleagues or clients – and how you go about influencing them.

How to reply

You could clarify whether the interviewer is thinking about a particular type of person – client, colleague or anyone in general life. Try to come up with an example that shows your ability to win someone round to your way of thinking. The outcome, as ever, should be positive. You might talk about how you try to manage the other person's expectations. For example, if you once had a difficult client, known for making excessive demands, you could talk about how you went about managing their expectations, clearly establishing what was expected of you and then planning how you were going to deliver on what was agreed.

Sample answer

When I was promoted to my current role, the person I was replacing warned me about a particular member of the team who seemed to resent authority and was in danger of facing disciplinary action. I decided to discuss his aspirations and concerns formally early on, before we had a run-in. I found that this person was frustrated because his role had been changed without his consent in a way that didn't allow him to use his skills effectively. I saw a way that we could rejig the department and gave him new responsibility and ownership of certain analytical tasks where he could really shine. He repaid my faith in him and he has just been nominated for employee of the month.

What motivates you?

The interviewer's aim

To find out whether you are self-motivated or need lots of input from managers, and whether you are compatible with the management style of the interviewer and the organization.

How to reply

Use any information you have picked up from your research, or during the interview so far, that suggests the factors you should highlight; these should clearly be motivations that complement the organization's style or goals.

If you know the company is currently number two in its market, but aiming to overtake the leader, you could talk about the thrill of helping your employing company beat the competition and become the acknowledged leader of its sector. If quality of service rather than volume is most important to the organization, you could talk about how you are motivated by trying to do the best job you can. If there is a culture of internal promotion, you could highlight the fact that you are motivated by helping young, inexperienced people learn how to do a job well. You might simply say you are motivated by being recognized for a job well done, even if that recognition comes in the form of just a simple thank-you from your boss; you realized the importance of this last week when your line manager thanked you in person for sorting out a rush delivery to a valued client which meant you had to work late on a Friday night.

How would you describe your work ethic?

The interviewer's aim

To get an insight into your work philosophy and whether that fits with the culture of the organization. This can be a tricky concept to answer if you haven't thought about it already, so it can make some unprepared interviewees feel under pressure.

How to reply

You might want to clarify what the interviewer is getting at – your attitude to work, or your moral code when at work? Clearly you want to dwell on positive aspects of your nature. For example, your attitude to work is that it is an important and stimulating part of your life. It offers opportunities for self-development and to work alongside other motivated people. However, you believe that it should be balanced with an active life outside the office.

If you are stressing your moral code, you might talk about the need for integrity or honesty when dealing with fellow workers. Have ready some examples of when your attitudes were tested in some way – perhaps you defended someone because you felt it was the right thing to do, even though this displeased head office, which was looking for easy scalps after some corporate disappointment.

How would your work colleagues describe you?

The interviewer's aim

To find out how you fit into a team and how you work with other people. Are you the giver, the taker, the leader, the follower, the conciliator, the provocateur, the calm one, the dramatic one?

How to reply

Try to identify, before attending the interview, the type of person that the organization is looking for to fill this particular role; you can then emphasize that aspect of your personality during the interview. Think about what you know about the organization to which you are applying; stress the qualities you have that you think offer the closest match to the organization's culture, as well as to the needs of the role in question.

In addition, remember that most modern roles involve teamwork and the sharing of information. With the spread of open-plan offices, your ability to interact effectively with other people is perhaps more important than ever before. So your answer should suggest that you can and do get on with others.

How would your boss describe you?

The interviewer's aim

To see whether you can talk about yourself relatively objectively. This also gives you the chance to quote a third-party source in support of your positive attributes.

How to reply

This should be easier than the question about how your colleagues describe you, since you should be able to refer to recent performance appraisals. Be sensible and dwell on the positive content, although you may feel it shows balance to refer to an area identified for improvement, stressing how you are already addressing it.

Sample answer

The most recent feedback I received from my boss was in my annual appraisal six months ago. This was significantly influenced by the work I had done on introducing a new training policy throughout the firm. In my appraisal my boss praised the way I had handled the cross-departmental consultation process. He was also impressed with the way I negotiated competitive rates with an external training provider, having arranged a competitive tender between three firms. He said my approach showed me to be efficient, thorough and able to handle complex tasks, ensuring they were completed against an agreed but tight deadline.

There was one area where we agreed I could try to improve, and that was on my use of internal memos. He suggested I try to be slightly more concise and use more bullet points to flag up the key action points. I have since started to do this, and just last week my boss complemented me on my improved communication style.

Tell me about yourself

The interviewer's aim

If asked at the start of the interview, the question may suggest that the interviewer is unprepared and can't remember much about you! Of course, it may be asked deliberately to see how focused you are or whether you are a chatterbox who would ramble on at length to customers or clients.

If asked at the end, the question indicates that the interviewer would like to know more about what makes you tick as a person outside, as well as inside, the office.

How to reply

If asked at the start of the interview, you are being given complete control over what you say. The danger is that it is so open an invitation to talk that you will go on too long and bore your interviewer. You should avoid rambling! It is probably sensible to clarify what the interviewer is looking for: 'Would you like me to give you a brief summary of my educational qualifications and career history?'

Make a real effort to be brief. You might want to start your answer by explaining what your current job entails. Then give a brief career history (which explains how you came to your current job) and finally close with what attracts you to the vacant position. Throughout your answer, focus on your experience and attributes that make you suitable for the available role.

If the interviewer asks you to talk about yourself at the end of the interview, use the opportunity to paint a picture of yourself as a well-rounded individual. How do you define yourself outside the office? You can refer to your family and your (noncontentious) interests – all are important elements that can bring you to life in the interviewer's eyes.

What makes you laugh?

The interviewer's aim

To find out just a little more about what makes you tick.

How to reply

You don't want to refer to anything that involves a joke at the expense of other people. You could suggest a form of humour (slapstick) or a particular comedian or a comic film. Your answer is unlikely to win or lose you the job (unless you name a notoriously offensive comedian, for example!) so just try to be yourself.

Describe your ideal job

The interviewer's aim

To find out how well your aspirations match the reality of the job on offer.

How to reply

Make sure you don't describe something completely different from the job vacancy. Take into account anything you know about the culture of the organization and try to build that into the answer. Try to phrase your answer in a way that suggests how your ideal job would enable you to benefit the organization, not just yourself. For example, you might say that one characteristic of your ideal job would be the potential to take on responsibility and find ways to add value to the organization, perhaps by leading a team implementing performance measures throughout all departments.

Where will you be in five years' time?

The interviewer's aim

The interviewer is trying to find out about your levels of ambition, your ability to think ahead, whether you have a structured career plan and whether applying for this job fits logically into that plan.

How to reply

You need to phrase your answer in such a way that applying for this job makes logical sense in terms of your career plan. Then, if you really want the job in question, your reply depends on whether you think the recruiter is looking for someone with great ambitions to move on in perhaps two years, or whether someone with longer staying power is required. Both situations could occur.

If someone with long-term commitment is required, you could be shooting yourself in the foot if you say you'd like two promotions and to be heading for the recruiter's job in five years' time. In that case you could say something along the lines of 'I've been through a series of fairly rapid promotions in the last five years and so looking ahead, I feel a period of consolidation is appropriate'. Of course, if you are really ambitious, it may be better to be honest because if you got the job, you could find yourself becoming frustrated if you weren't encouraged to develop the role or your own abilities.

An alternative might be to try the politician's style of answer.

> I don't honestly know where I will be in five years' time; that clearly depends on a number of factors, including this job. But, I am the kind of person who sets medium-term goals. I previously set myself the goal of becoming a finance director within five years, and I achieved that with a year to spare. I find setting such goals helps me to achieve potentially more than I could do otherwise, or to achieve it faster.

Completing your own agenda

Kickstart Tip

Throughout the interview your aim should be to convey your strengths and suitability for the position. Never blame the interviewer for not asking you the right questions to give you the platform to talk about your strengths. You should be prepared to do this, whatever the questions.

But what if there is one major strength that you haven't managed to bring into the discussion, one you feel highly relevant to the role you are applying for? The interviewer reaches the end of his interrogation. His final question is likely to be, 'Do you have any questions for me?' You could reply 'No, thank you', shake hands with the interviewer and rush off as fast as possible. This won't make a very impressive conclusion to the interview, however. It could actually damage any positive impression you have made. You need to have some questions up your sleeve. But before asking them, take a moment to bring out the area of your strengths not yet highlighted.

> ### Kickstart Tip
>
> Think of this 'Any questions?' section of the interview rather as 'Any other business?' and use it to talk about issues of importance for you.

Say you are applying for an IT job. You believe there are four key areas of your experience that make you highly suitable. Three have come up in your answers – your strong technical knowledge, systems integration background and people-management ability. However, the fact that you can handle multi-site divisions has not been mentioned.

Before your first question, you could just say you would like to mention one other factor which you believe relevant to your job application. Then briefly outline your experience in managing the IT systems for the 20-site business where you currently work. You might use this topic as the foundation for your first question. You could perhaps ask how the business ensures effective communication or team-building between staff at the different sites.

Questioning the interviewer effectively

As we have said, interviewers expect to be asked questions by candidates. A lack of questions suggests lack of interest in the organization and the job.

When preparing questions to ask, bear in mind that your questions should:

- emphasize your enthusiasm for the role;
- play up to your own strengths, rather than drawing attention to any potential weaknesses;
- reveal your knowledge and experience; and
- indicate that you have researched the organization and the job role.

Clearly your questions should do this in a subtle manner. For example, you could highlight your knowledge by asking a question that focuses on some detailed aspect of the organization's activities or marketplace.

Pick your questions well; this closing section of the interview gives you a powerful opportunity to emphasize how suitable you are for the vacancy and the organization.

Good questions to ask interviewers

Our research questionnaire asked recruiters what questions they expected candidates to ask, or questions they were impressed by. These fall into a number of themes and should give you some ideas of topics that might be appropriate for you.

The particular job role

- What would my specific responsibilities be in this particular aspect of the role? (For example, new systems implementation, staff training, etc.)
- How does this role contribute to fulfilling the company's strategy?
- How do the reporting lines work?
- Why did this position become vacant?
- What qualities do you believe are most important for this role?
- What do you think is the biggest challenge in the role?
- Are any specific changes anticipated for this role or the department in the near future?
- What are the key challenges facing the department? (e.g. managing workloads, staff turnover)

Colleagues

- Who would I be working with on a daily or regular basis?
- Who are the key people within the immediate team?
- What is the average length of service of people in the department?
- Would it be possible to meet a few of my potential colleagues at some stage?

Performance measurement

- What would I need to have achieved by the end of three, six or 12 months for you to feel my appointment had been a success?
- How would my performance be measured?
- What is the performance appraisal process?

Training and development

- What happened to the last person in this role?
- Do you expect someone to stay in this position for a certain length of time?
- Is there a typical career progression expected after fulfilling this position?
- How are training courses chosen?
- How is training tailored to reflect individual needs?
- What induction procedures are there?
- What options are there for developing this role?

The recruiting organization

- Please tell me more about the company's objectives in this area? (e.g. environmental protection, global development, e-commerce, etc.)
- There's been a lot of debate in the press about the challenges faced by this sector. Apart from this company's publicly stated aim of doing x and y, are any more strategic responses being considered?
- Where does the organization expect to be in five years' time?
- How is the department expected to develop in the short term?
- Can you give me an example of how the organization lives up to its cultural reputation of being supportive of staff development?
- How would you describe the culture or working style within this department?
- What contribution does the organization make to society as a whole?

The line manager's or recruiter's career history

- How long have you been with this organization?
- Why have you stayed with it?
- How has the organization met your own expectations?

It's reasonable to ask two or three such questions, but don't try to keep the interviewer talking too long. You want to highlight your knowledge and enthusiasm, not your insensitivity to other people's time schedules!

Chapter summary: key points

- Prepare for your interview by rehearsing answers to likely questions.
- As a minimum, if you are short of time, practise answers to the interviewers' top ten questions listed below.
- Use real examples from your working life to illustrate how you apply your expertise and skills in practice.
- Refer to appraisals and performance reviews for evidence of your ability.
- Remember to illustrate your softer skills as well as practical or technical ones.
- Don't waffle.
- Think about what the interviewer is trying to get at by asking the question.
- Prepare some questions to ask the interviewer.
- Take control of the final 'Any questions?' section to stress any of your qualities not yet highlighted but relevant to the vacancy.
- Make sure the questions you ask highlight your knowledge of the employer and its sector, as well as your ability and enthusiasm.

Kickstart Tip

The Top Ten Interview Questions
The favourite questions asked by interviewers responding to our survey:

- What is the most difficult or challenging experience you have had to deal with?
- What is your greatest career achievement?
- What was your biggest mistake or disappointment?
- Why do you think you are suited to this position?
- What are your weaknesses?
- What are your main strengths?
- What are your ambitions: where will you be in 5 to 10 years' time?
- How would your colleagues or boss describe you?
- Why are you leaving your current job?
- What do you like or dislike about your current job?

Chapter 15

Passing the Tests

Depending on your sector, specialism and seniority, you may have to undergo a variety of tests designed to ensure you have the appropriate ability, personality or skills for the role you seek.

In our survey, well over 80 per cent of human resources professionals and two-thirds of recruitment professionals said they used tests when recruiting.

Who gets tested?

Many people assume that tests are most often used for recruiting graduates. However, our research found that testing is potentially used for appointments at all management levels, although slightly more frequently for senior and middle management roles.

At junior levels, tests are often held after the initial paper screening of applications, in order to identify a shortlist of candidates for final interview. At more senior levels, testing may occur after the first-round interview and be used to distinguish between candidates already on the shortlist.

Types of tests

Recruiters use a variety of tests to help them make appointment decisions. The key types are:

- Psychometric tests focused on personality: designed to identify the kind of personality and behavioural style of the applicant;
- Psychometric tests focused on aptitude: designed to test the individual's innate abilities and/or potential to be trained;
- Skills tests: these test current, actual skill levels; and
- Knowledge-based tests: assessing levels of applied knowledge.

These tests may be extremely short – taking just five minutes to complete – or they could last for half an hour or longer. In any case, they must be taken seriously; your performance has a direct impact on your chances in winning a job offer.

Psychometric tests

According to our research, psychometric testing of personality or aptitude is the most common type of test used in the recruitment process – used by half of our survey respondents.

- **Personality**
  Candidates are generally required to complete multiple-choice questionnaires asking how they react or behave in certain situations, what kinds of beliefs they hold and their preferences or attitudes. The questionnaire aims to develop a picture of how you relate to other people, how you deal with your own and other people's emotions, what motivates you, your working style and your general outlook on life.

  Obviously there can be no right or wrong answers. However, the job specification will generally be associated with a number of personality characteristics, which will be compared to your personality profile as produced by your answers. Your responses on the questionnaire may also be referred to during a subsequent interview; you might be asked to explain, using examples taken from your past experiences and actions, why you said you would behave in a particular way, or to talk more about your motivations.

- **Aptitude**
  Aptitude tests can take many forms. In our survey, 21 per cent of respondents used numeracy tests, which can include charts and graphs, while other common forms included verbal or logical reasoning and spatial reasoning (involving abstract shapes).

  These tests are usually administered under exam conditions with a strict time limit, and candidates can easily run out of time. You therefore need to apply sound exam technique. Read the instructions carefully and make sure you understand what is required. If you have any questions, ask before the test starts.

  This is particularly important where negative marking for wrong answers is being used. For example, some marking procedures might deduct one mark for every three questions answered incorrectly, while others might take off a mark for each wrong answer. If the instructions for your test say something like 'Wrong answers will count against you' it's worth finding out exactly how the marking works.

  Once you understand the marking system, you can decide your test strategy. If there is no negative marking, then clearly you should try to answer every question

– guessing where necessary. Even if you have no idea which of four options is correct, by picking one you have a 25 per cent chance of success. Where possible, make fast judgements to rule out obviously incorrect choices; you can then make an informed guess between the remaining options and so improve your odds.

If negative marking applies, you might want to be a little more cautious. However, bear in mind that every question you read but don't answer still carries a cost in terms of time used up without any hope of adding to your score. If you have a choice of four answers and can quickly eliminate two, but have no idea which of the others is correct, it is still probably worth taking the 50:50 chance and having a guess, even where negative marking is used.

Finally, experience shows that when candidates change their original answers, 60 per cent of the time they are changing a correct answer to an incorrect one. This means you should try to trust your instincts and only change your first answer if you are 100 per cent convinced you made a mistake.

Kickstart Tip

Unlike personality tests, aptitude tests *do* have right and wrong answers and your final score will reflect not only your ability to answer *correctly*, but also the *speed* of your answers.

Candidates' scores are measured against a standardized population of people who have previously taken the same test, enabling the recruiters to assess your ability in relation to others. Aptitude tests are potentially more important than personality tests, where there is usually greater subjectivity as to the type of personality required for a particular role. If your aptitude test results suggest you don't have the potential to be trained to the necessary skill level, you won't be offered the job.

Skills tests

These attempt to assess the current level of skills attained by applicants. The type of skills being assessed will be determined by the job applied for, but common forms of such test include:

- in-tray exercises – where your ability to prioritize work according to its importance will be assessed;
- presentations – alone or in groups, to test your spoken communication ability, self-confidence and creativity in preparing supporting materials;
- other communication and literacy tests – perhaps by letter or memo, or some form of group discussion;
- role plays – to assess your behavioural style in different situations; and
- case studies – which measure your ability to absorb information and suggest appropriate, sensible actions or resolutions.

When completing such exercises, always try to fulfil the brief you are given as closely as possible. Try not to waste time on unimportant issues. Be clear what each exercise is trying to achieve, and act accordingly. For example, avoid silly mistakes such as spelling errors in written tests. Participate fully in all group activities, but don't be afraid to demonstrate your own initiative and defend your own opinions.

Knowledge-based tests

Knowledge-based tests tend to take the form of multiple-choice questions. In this way they are similar to aptitude tests, but they differ in that they are measuring acquired knowledge rather than trainability.

They are particularly prevalent in the IT sector where they might be used, for example, to assess a candidate's level of applied knowledge in a particular programming language. They are also used in the administration arena, testing applied expertise in using word-processing or spreadsheet packages.

Preparing to take the tests

Throughout this book we have stressed the need to prepare yourself thoroughly. The same goes for preparing to take recruitment tests. Don't leave your performance in the tests to chance. You should make an effort to:

- find out exactly what tests you will be asked to complete;
- practise similar tests where possible; and
- try to be in good mental and physical shape on the day.

Find out what tests you will face

If you know you are going to be required to complete a series of tests, ask the recruiter what kind of tests these will be. Some recruiters will even supply a leaflet in advance that includes sample questions of the type you will be expected to answer.

Practise if possible

There is some debate about whether practising tests really has much impact on the results: psychologists tend to believe that practising has relatively little impact, whereas testing specialists believe people can improve their scores.

The bottom line is that there can be no harm in maximizing your chances of performing well and practising typical tests in advance. For example, many aptitude tests that assess reasoning or spatial awareness use common forms of question. The first time you see them, even if you have a high aptitude in that area, you inevitably go through a learning process in understanding the test and the solution. If you have seen similar tests before, you should be able to speed up your performance in choosing an answer, complete a higher number of questions and increase your test score as a result.

You should be able to find a selection of test booklets stocked in your local bookshop. Even if the types of questions you are given aren't exactly the same, practising answering questions under time pressure is a useful experience of you haven't had to take a formal test of any sort for some years.

Be in your best shape

Remember, you only get one chance to do well in these tests. Unlike school exams, you won't normally be able to resit them. Unless there are particularly unusual circumstances, allowing you another go at the tests would give you an unfair advantage over the other applicants and so recruiters will resist this.

Therefore, you need to make sure you give yourself every chance of doing your best on the day. Try to be well-rested after a good night's sleep to give your brain cells their best chance of maximizing their performance.

Apply the same approach as you would to an ordinary interview. Double-check where you need to be and when, and work out how to get there. Make sure you arrive with plenty of time to spare so that you can settle your thoughts and focus on the task in hand.

Assessment centres

The tests we have described may be applied individually. However, some recruiters decide to put their applicants through a series of tests and run 'assessment centres' in order to do so. Although not common according to our survey – just 4 per cent of our respondents said they used assessment centres as part of the recruitment process – recruiters say that the use of assessment centres is on the increase. They can be used when only one person is being recruited, or where multiple positions of the same kind need to be filled.

Timing and format

Tests undertaken at assessment centres are most often applied to applicants already on a shortlist and are used to influence the final appointment decision. However, they can vary significantly in content and style. Some, for example, may last for just half a day, while others stretch over two days involving a night's stay. As well as the tests and exercises that you will be asked to complete, the schedule may include presentations by representatives of the recruiting organization. The assessment centre therefore provides an opportunity not only for you to demonstrate your skills and ability, but also for you to learn more about the potential employer.

Testing variety

A major idea behind assessment centres is that they try to mirror the key competencies associated with the positions to be filled. In-tray exercises and psychometric tests are therefore common elements of the assessment centre process, as well as traditional interviews.

When there are a group of shortlisted candidates attending the assessment centre, tests that involve group activities are also extremely common. For example, you may have to work with other candidates to prepare a presentation, develop a business strategy or come up with a solution to a case-study problem. Your performance in such activities will be judged not only on your own individual brain power and ability, but also on your skill as a teamworker. Assessors will be drawing conclusions as to whether you are a leader or a follower, someone who dominates quieter group members or someone who tries to draw out contributions from everyone.

Constant assessment

Even between activities – such as over coffee or lunch – you will be assessed. How well do you interact with other people? Are you the nervous type? Are you bullish? There isn't necessarily a right or wrong way to behave, since your recruiters may be looking for different types of personality, depending on the role in question. However, it goes without saying that you should remember to behave with courtesy towards your fellow candidates and your assessors. Try to mix with all your fellow applicants and with any employees and potential colleagues you meet, showing your enthusiasm and asking questions.

Stress management

Attending an assessment centre can be stressful, given that you are facing in-depth scrutiny by your recruiters over a longer period than you would undergo with just a standard interview. In addition, some assessment centres build in extra stress as part of the process for judging candidate's suitability for the job. You may be subjected to extreme time pressure, for example, when completing activities or be challenged robustly on what you are doing and why. Mike Dodd, managing director of Academy HR Services, a specialist assessment organization that runs assessment centres for recruiting employers, says:

> Assessment centres are designed to mirror the competencies in the jobs being filled; they try to establish and assess those traits that are predictive of success in the role. They do have the potential to create a fairly pressurized situation, if that is appropriate. We have had situations where people have walked out from the assessment centre because of the pressure, although it's unusual for that to happen. If it does, it suggests the assessment centre is doing its job properly because the position being filled is a high-pressure one and the candidate wouldn't have been able to take it.

If you are attending an assessment centre, try to remember that the situation is merely a simulation; take it seriously, but remind yourself that it is not real life. That said, if you find yourself becoming too stressed by the whole process, then perhaps the role you have applied for really is not for you, given that the features of the assessment centre are tailored to mirror the characteristics of the role being filled.

However, the same general rule applies to attending assessment centres as to attending interviews: while you are there, you should not be trying to take a decision about whether you do or do not want the job. Apply all your attention and energy to performing to the best of your ability. Think about whether you want the job, and can handle the stress, afterwards.

Afterwards

It is hard to perform at your peak throughout the duration of an entire assessment centre attendance. At the time, don't focus on what went wrong but only on doing your best in the next activity. However, afterwards, when you are safely away from the assessment centre site, it may be worth spending a little time considering how things went and identifying anything you could try to do better.

Make notes of any key points to remind yourself the next time you are about to go through the same process. Think about any feedback you received during the assessment centre visit and ask yourself whether you need to adjust your behaviour in any way. Consider whether you have learnt anything more about the organization, perhaps about its management style, that influences how keen you are to work there.

Kickstart Tip

Don't forget to write down the names of the employees and candidates you met who you may meet again at a later stage – perhaps at a final interview or, if you are ultimately successful in your application, after you have joined the organization.

Chapter summary: key points

- The use of tests in the recruitment process is increasing.
- Psychometric tests aim to establish your personality type and levels of aptitude or trainability in different areas.
- Other activities (such as in-tray exercises, presentations and case studies) assess current, actual skill levels.
- Tests may involve individual working as well as group exercises to see how you interact with others in reality.
- When taking timed tests, check the marking system and apply the appropriate answering technique.
- Find out in advance what tests you will be required to take.
- Practise similar tests in advance.
- Try to be in your best shape on the day of the tests.
- Assessment centres are being used increasingly to fill either individual or numerous positions, even at senior management levels.
- Assessment centres can last over two days and combine a range of tests and activities chosen to simulate the particular job specification.
- Remember that you are being assessed at all times, even when chatting informally with other candidates.
- Show enthusiasm at all times.
- Be prepared for stressful moments.
- Afterwards make notes on how you think you did, areas you could improve, information you discovered about the employer and the names of any people – candidates and assessors – you met during the process.

Chapter 16

Negotiating the Best Job Offer

The aim of the job interview is to gain a job offer. Once that goal has been achieved, you then have the luxury of being able to decide whether you actually want to take the job. If you decide you do, then the serious business of negotiating the terms of the offer can begin.

Assessing the offer

When you achieve your interview objective and find yourself celebrating a job offer, you deserve to pat yourself on the back. You have presented yourself to a potential employer and met their criteria for ability, skills, personal communication and so on. You should quite rightly enjoy the thrill of success.

You should also keep your head.

You have been offered the job, but do you really want it?

Be aware of the emotional element that inevitably comes to play in assessing the offer. Try not to get carried away. Unless you really hate your current job and can't wait to leave it, or you really detest the job-hunting process, or you don't expect to receive as good an offer elsewhere, there is no reason why you have to take the first job offer that comes along. The fact you have been successful with this job application suggests you have what employers look for and could well expect to receive a number of other offers, especially if the offer you receive comes after only a couple of interviews.

If you are to make a rational decision about whether the offered job is right for you, you need to consider issues such as:

- How well does the job on offer meet your original job-hunting aims?
- Does it fit well into your overall career blueprint?
- Would you be working in a quality sector and organization?
- Is there a close cultural fit between yourself and the organization?
- Are any of the terms of the offered role substantially different to the terms you presently enjoy?
- Have all your questions and concerns been adequately answered?

At the start of this book we suggested that a successful job search is founded on a degree of self-analysis – what are you really looking for in your new job? What kind of organization and role would suit you? Assessing the offer therefore involves more than simply considering the adequacy of the pay packet.

Original aims

> ### Kickstart Tip
>
> If you wrote down at the start of your job hunt what you were looking for in your next role, dig those thoughts out now and compare the potential of the offered job against your stated requirements. The closer the fit, the less likely you are to feel disappointed and restless after just two months in the new position. An exact match may be too much to hope for; a close match is definitely worth considering.

There may be some requirements that are essentials – perhaps minimum holiday time to enable you to stay in touch with your family. Remind yourself what those were.

Identifying mismatches in essential areas will indicate where you could try negotiating improvements in the package offered. If the employer won't negotiate, then you simply have to decide whether these remain essential items for you or whether you are prepared to give them up, at least in the short term.

Your career blueprint

One factor that you should specifically consider is how well the offered position fits into the desired blueprint of your career. Is this the next step that develops your customer-facing skills and so fills that glaring gap in your current work experience?

> ### Kickstart Tip
>
> Try to imagine where the natural next step from this job would be, and whether that would continue to take you in a desirable direction. If the job appears to be sidelining you in a niche that really doesn't grab you as much as the broader, more commercial role you have just been filling, perhaps you should avoid it.

Throughout the job-hunting and career process you need to keep your mind open to the issue of what skills you are developing, how each role you fill adds to your marketability. If you cannot see how the new job adds anything in these areas, be wary.

Sometimes an employer may offer a job with a view to being able to move you into a more interesting role at a certain date. Such offers can be particularly hard to judge. What rights do you have if the promised other role never appears? You might want to gain reassurance by asking whether other people have had similar promises made and whether they were kept. If the promised role is currently filled by someone else, can you speak to them to see whether they are really planning to move in a year's time? What about other internal candidates for that role? Might you have to go through an internal interview process all over again?

If you are not absolutely satisfied by further enquiries, you could try asking for the insertion of a specific term in your contract covering the issue. However, this will need to be carefully drafted and employers often do not want to commit themselves in this way.

Quality control

Before you applied to the target organization, you should have made an initial judgement about its quality and the strength of the sector in which it operates. However, as you proceeded with your application and attended interviews, new information may have come to light. It's worth double-checking that you are still in agreement with your initial judgement. For example, you knew the company was growing fast; has your experience in dealing with it reassured you as to management's ability in managing that growth?

Cultural fit

Having gone through the interview process you should also have formed an impression of the pervasive management style inside the organization. How does that fit with your own temperament and style? What if the job role is perfect, exactly matching your job search criteria, but the company itself worries you in that you don't think your personality really fits in?

> ### Kickstart Tip
>
> Experience suggests that the wrong job in the right company often turns out to be the right job in the long run. If the organization fits you like a glove, then even if the initial role is not what you consider an ideal fit, nevertheless you will probably thrive in the organization and will subsequently be able to move into a role that does match your demands.

The alternative can be frustrating. You may find the right job, but if the culture in the organization does not suit you, the chances are you will dissipate too much energy banging up against it. Choosing an organization is like choosing a life partner; if you don't have shared values and a common outlook, you are likely to find the experience of living – or working – together a frustrating one.

Minimizing the risk and checking contractual terms

While acknowledging the element of risk in changing jobs, recognize that risk is the flip side of opportunity. Fortune favours the bold. Taking all risk out of your career could only happen if you spent your life working in the same organization, with the same people, doing exactly the same thing until you retire. How boring does that sound? In any case, organizations and colleagues will change around you.

Not all risks are the same, though. You can take informed risks (the sensible option) on uninformed risks (bad, bad, bad).

If you have applied the solid, research approach to your job-hunting process, you should already know a fair bit about the organization you are considering joining. However, as we discuss below, after receiving the offer, you might want to go in and talk with your peers and line manager to form a fuller picture of what the working life is really like in the organization and of your potential role.

Once you see the job contract you should certainly seek clarification of any elements that appear unclear. For example, your offer letter may contain a reference to a probationary period that you must complete before your new job is guaranteed. If so, what exactly are the criteria you must meet to pass the probationary test? Who decides on your performance? How often have people been thrown out in the past after just three months' trial?

You should also make sure you understand how all the employee benefits are administered. How much flexibility is there in choosing between benefits? If there is a promise for you to join any particular benefits scheme, such as a pension or medical scheme, make sure time limits are set for when you will join or when the benefits schemes will be set up; you should clarify that, should these time limits be breached, you will receive benefits in another manner, such as cash or a payment to a personal scheme.

If you have to complete a probationary period, make sure all the benefits that go with the job start on day one or, if they do not, they are at least backdated to your start date once your probationary period is over and you are confirmed as a full-time employee.

When looking through your contract, keep an eye open for any 'restrictive convenant' clauses. These are used by employers to try to restrict what their employees do during or after their employment with the organization. The main types of restrictive covenant try to restrict an employee's ability to give away confidential information, moonlight on the job, work for direct competitors (non-competition), poach other employees or try to attract business from the company's customers once the employee has left (non-solicitation).

If you spot such clauses in your contract be aware that they are actually quite hard to enforce in the courts, particularly non-competition clauses which tend to be relevant only for senior employees in any case. As for non-solicitation clauses, these probably won't affect you unless you work in a customer-facing role.

You shouldn't just ignore restrictive convenants, however, if you earn under £20,000 and are at a relatively junior level, try simply asking for the employer to remove any such clauses from your contract. If this request is refused, tell the employer you want it to pay for legal advice so you can check these contractual terms out. If this is refused, you may just have to take a decision on how likely you are to ever be in a position where these clauses could restrict your options significantly but try to take as much advice as you can from either a solicitor or a reputable HR consultant.

If you are a more senior executive, it may well be worth taking expert legal advice. This should at least give you an idea of how enforceable the restrictive covenants could be. It may also help you to negotiate the terms. For example, you should at least ensure that any clients or contacts you made before joining the new employer are outside the scope of the restrictive covenants because these contacts were not generated on the company's time. If the company refuses to alter the contract terms in any way, you at least have an idea where you are likely to stand if you breach them. It also gives you an idea of the flexibility of the organization. Jonathan R Ebsworth, partner with Reid Minty, Solicitors, offers the following advice:

> In most normal circumstances you should not sign a contract which you may not want to comply with. However, knowledge is everything when dealing with restrictive covenants and many employers are not adept at dealing with them properly. 'I am afraid you must agree this clause, it is the Company's standard restrictive clause', is often what you will hear, but this is a contradiction in terms. There can be no such thing, as each person's case will be different. If the 'standard clause' goes beyond what is reasonable and necessary to protect an employer's business interests it will be void and you will be able to sign it knowing that you need not comply with it.

Seeking answers from appropriate people

If you have significant queries about your potential new job, now is the time to request another meeting at the employer's offices. So far you may have had two interviews where you have been focusing on selling yourself and where you have not been fully in control of the situation. The interviewer has had the whip hand.

> **Kickstart Tip**
>
> Now you have the job offer, the balance of power has swung over to your side and you can go back with your eyes focused on seeing whether the organization really meets your standards.

A sensible option is to ask to meet some of your potential peer group. You want to have the opportunity to talk freely, out of earshot of your previous interviewer or potential line manager, and ask questions about what it is really like to work in that organization. Do reporting lines flow freely? What is the immediate boss really like as a manager? How long have people been with the company? Is there anything they don't like about it? If at all possible, try to talk to the individual you would be replacing; this can give you the best insight into the challenges and stimuli of the job.

A meeting with your potential immediate boss (who may also have been your interviewer) can be useful. You can ask questions you were perhaps nervous about asking before, or seek reassurance on answers you have already received, perhaps concerning career break options, training courses or potential for expanding the basic role in certain areas, such as taking a larger part in staff management.

If the line manager can't answer, you might want to try and squeeze in a session with personnel too. This may be a wise policy in any case. It is not unknown for new recruits to be told one thing by a line manager eager to get them on board, only to find out that the initial information was incorrect. You may not have been told a deliberate lie; the manager may have believed his answer to be truthful, not knowing that company policy was about to change. If in any doubt, check with the real authority on any issue. If the answer is pertinent to your decision as to whether to join the organization or not, then you had better check it is correct. Don't just believe what you want to believe.

Checklists of questions to ask after receiving the job offer

Having an informal chat with people within the organization you are considering joining could provide useful information before you make up your mind whether the job is right for you. The sample questions below may or may not be relevant, depending on your particular job role and the organization you are considering joining.

Whatever you ask, try to phrase questions in ways that avoid Yes or No answers; How or What questions should trigger more informative replies than questions starting with 'Do you. . .' as in 'Do you like it here?'

Above all, be polite. If you are talking to a potential peer, it's highly likely that this person's opinion of you will get back to the boss. And if you are going to work with them, you want that impression to be positive.

Questions for your prospective boss

- Who exactly do I report to?
- Who will be involved in my performance assessments?
- Is there a probationary period and if so, how long is it and how is my performance assessed?
- What initial training will I get?
- Who are the other members of the team I would be working with?

- What software packages does the department use?
- How often does the team work overtime?
- How long have you been in this department/company/organization?
- Where did the person I am replacing move on to and why?
- What factors might affect the actual bonus I receive?
- How much travel is realistically likely to be involved?
- How many women are there in the senior management team?
- What promotion prospects might be available in future?

Questions for your peers/the person you are replacing

- How long have you worked here?
- What made you join?
- How have your expectations been met?
- What kinds of projects have you worked on?
- What is the most interesting part of your work here?
- What do you like best about the company/organization?
- Are there any downsides to working here?
- How many people have left the department recently?
- The hours are supposed to be 9 to 5. What are they really like?
- Do you ever work weekends?
- What's the boss really like to work for?
- Tell me about the personalities in this team.
- What is the atmosphere like in the office?
- Are there any personality clashes?
- Do people socialize after hours and is that expected?
- How much support do you get in terms of training and personal development?
- Why did the person I'm replacing leave?
- The bonus scheme looks good, but does it live up to expectations?
- Do female staff members tend to return to their old jobs after maternity leave?

Questions for human resources

- What is the average time that staff stay with the organization?
- Are there any formal policies concerning internal promotion?

- Can you talk me through the company benefits open to me?
- Are there any qualifying periods that apply before I am eligible for these benefits?
- How are pay reviews organized?
- What training programme does the company have?
- Can I request training in particular areas if I feel that would benefit both me and the organization?
- Can you take me through the contract I will be asked to sign?

Asking for more money

You might like the offered job description, but does the pay package meet your needs? In Chapter 13, Interview Savvy we advised that any discussion of money, specifically the kind of salary you are looking for, should be avoided during the interview process. In our survey questionnaire 57 per cent of HR professionals said they felt the appropriate stage to discuss remuneration was *after* the job offer had been made.

However, half of the headhunters questioned and over half of line managers felt that raising the subject at the second interview was appropriate. Of course, this timing is what they may see as in their best interests; at that stage they are in the more powerful position because the job offer has not yet been made. As far as you are concerned, your negotiating position is strongest after you have been offered the job with the employer, so you are best keeping your powder dry on the subject of pay and benefits until the recruiters have committed themselves to you.

Kickstart Tip

The impression you should be giving right up until the point where you receive the offer is that you are prepared to work for nothing – it's the thrill of the job, the challenges in store, the potential to contribute to the organization and develop your own talents that primarily attract you. You are inspired and motivated by the holy trinity of Challenge, Opportunity and Responsibility.

Of course, while this may be the impression you are trying to create, it is unlikely to be true! Unless you have independent means, your pay certainly will matter to you.

If the organization wants to offer you a position, then it clearly values your skills and potential to add value; it should therefore be prepared to pay you to share your skills.

It's OK to ask for more

The number of people who actually accept the first offer the new employer makes is surprisingly high. The majority of successful applicants generally don't try to negotiate any increase at all. However, there is no reason why more people shouldn't try to obtain some uplift on the original offer.

Kickstart Tip

The organization won't think any the worse of you if you come back with a slightly higher request or one that includes specific terms, perhaps involving particular benefits. In our survey, just 11 per cent of respondents said they were put off by a candidate asking them to increase the initial salary offer; the vast majority said it was no problem at all, if the request was justified or rational.

The new employer doesn't have to agree to your request. The answer may be 'No, the first offer is our best', but at least you know where you stand. If you don't ask you certainly won't get. And if you don't get precisely what you want, you may at least be offered some form of compromise. Perhaps you wanted an extra 2 per cent or 3 per cent on the offered salary. The request may be rejected, but perhaps instead of being made to wait a year for a pay review, you are offered a date six months ahead, with the specific provision that a possible pay rise will be considered if you deliver against certain agreed criteria. Maybe you will be offered a minimum guaranteed bonus or even a 'golden hello' in the form of a one-off, lump sum payment.

The recruiting organization may well have a fairly rigid staff-grading system or pay structure. In which case, trying to argue yourself into a grade for which you clearly do not qualify is likely to be an impossible task. On the other hand, you don't want to accept a grade and pay offer that puts you clearly on too low a level. Once established in the internal grading structure, it can be hard to make a corrective jump upwards. The higher you start, the higher you are likely to be placed on your next performance and pay review.

Preparing for negotiations

If you are to negotiate effectively, you need to have a proper understanding of the value of the package of salary and benefits being offered to you, and of the value of your current package. Remuneration packages have become increasingly flexible.

Stewart Rogers, Managing Director of the Rogers Partnership and an independent remuneration and organizational change consultant, says:

> Until the late 1980s employers tended to decide what the elements of the benefits package were; employees had no choice. However, they then began to introduce flexibility, offering a pool of benefits that employees could choose from. The latest trend is to offer a cash-only package, but this happens where employers have negotiated a range of preferential deals, say with insurance companies and so on. These employers are increasingly saying, 'The cost of your total remuneration package to us is this amount; if you want it all in cash, fine; or if you want to spend some of that on pensions, with the deals we have negotiated, that's your choice.

Deciding whether a salary and benefits package of this kind gives you an appropriate uplift can be achieved only if you fully understand the value of what you are receiving with your current employer. There could be many elements over and above your base salary. You need to take into account all the different elements that make up the total package.

Try to attach a financial value to items such as:

- employer's pension contributions;
- the company car or car allowance;
- paid leave;
- corporate perks such as gym membership;
- reimbursement of home telephone costs;
- private health insurance; and
- share options.

The process is more complicated if you have been receiving a significant part of your total pay as a year-end bonus or profit share. You may need to guess what you would be in line for if you were staying to the end of the current year.

Share options can also complicate matters. If you leave your job now, will you lose out on potentially valuable options, or is the stock doing so poorly that you have little to lose?

You should also be aware of any extra costs you might incur by taking up the job offer you have received. Will you have to move location and into an area with a higher cost of living, particularly in terms of higher house prices? If so, will your new employer help subsidize these relocation costs?

Kickstart Tip

The importance you place on the different elements of your remuneration package may, of course, shift over time. As you reach your mid-thirties, pensions issues will probably seem more critical than they did in your twenties. Be clear what elements offer you real value, as opposed to status value, although you are clearly free to decide that status is what matters to you most!

If you are unsure of the pay and benefits details, particularly concerning pensions issues, it may be worth calling your personal financial adviser for advice, if you have one. If you don't, this could be a good time to start taking advice on your personal finances.

Once you have considered all the different elements you can total them up to reveal the total value of your current package. This provides your opening reference point in negotiations with your potential new employer.

How much salary uplift is attainable?

When moving jobs, you should be aware that you can generally expect a higher salary increase than if you stayed put. Experience shows that the average pay rise for someone who stays with their current employer and keeps their nose clean is around 3–4 per cent.

Kickstart Tip

Our research found that the average salary increase offered to candidates was 9 per cent, with most offers representing an increase of either 5 per cent or 10 per cent. Almost one in five recruiters said they would offer a 15 per cent or 20 per cent increase.

In contrast, professional recruiters generally start from the assumption that an individual moving jobs will be looking for a salary at least 10 per cent higher than their current pay; at the most senior levels a salary uplift of 25 per cent is more the norm.

The more outstanding the candidate, the more flexibility organizations achieve in their pay offers.

Back-up material

As with every element of the job-hunting process, the more information you have to strengthen your side in negotiations, the better. In this case try to get hold of some pay and benefits data for your type of role and your industry. You may find that you have been underpaid by your past employer. In this case, using your current total pay package as your starting point could leave you short-changed. You should perhaps be trying for considerably more than the typical 10 per cent increase. If you have been using a recruitment consultancy, they should be able to give you a good idea of the market conditions and what you could reasonably expect to be offered. You can also make use of statistical data on market rates. Apart from your recruiting firm, if you are using one, other useful reference material may come from specialist pay and benefits organizations such as The Reward Group, Incomes Data Services or Towers Perrin (see Appendix for contact details). Organizations like these tend to conduct surveys fairly regularly and it should be relatively easy to get hold of relevant statistics.

Who should negotiate?

If you have been working with a recruitment consultancy or headhunter, then it is probably worth getting them to handle the opening round of negotiations. Specialist recruiters have the skills to be able to put your case effectively, so you may as well make the most of them. It can also help to avoid any embarrassment or the potential for a confrontational atmosphere between yourself and the new employer. If you are going to work there, you want to start on the best of terms – psychologically as well as financially.

Opening negotiations

The art of negotiation lies in reaching a compromise where both parties emerge feeling a winner. This means the final outcome may involve you meeting the employer halfway between their offer and your upper target.

Let's say you would be happy to receive a total package equivalent to a 10 per cent rise on what you currently receive, although an uplift of 20 per cent would really help with the new mortgage. However, the company makes you an offer equivalent to a 5 per cent rise. You have nothing to lose by trying for more.

The way to phrase the response would be to say first, how delighted you are to have received the offer. You have been very impressed with the organization during the applications and interview process and see exciting opportunities for yourself through working there. However, you are slightly disappointed at the size of the offer you have received.

You can then refer to your current package and the size of the rise you were looking for. Remember that the likelihood is that you will be job-hunting part-way through the year. Your next pay review with your current employer may be coming up soon. However, if you change jobs you will probably have to wait a year for your next review, so it is reasonable to expect a higher rise now.

Ongoing negotiations

Once you have responded to the initial salary package offer, indicating you would like to receive an increased offer, you have to wait for the organization to react. The result may be a flat refusal of any increase, a desired upward offer or a query as to what package you would be willing to accept.

Kickstart Tip

Never talk in terms of what you 'need'. You should phrase discussions in terms of what you are 'worth'. That value is inevitably determined by a combination of factors – your ability, the employer's need, the general economic environment and your discipline's scarcity value.

Negotiations may continue through several rounds before the organization reaches a point beyond which it moves no further, or where you feel an acceptable offer has been made. If at any stage the company is slow to respond, do not feel you have to just sit and wait for a reply. Unless the company has clearly indicated it wants to have a certain amount of time to respond, there is no harm in trying to keep up the momentum.

Throughout these negotiations, make sure you place your requests in a positive context and in a constructive and non-confrontational way, while stressing your enthusiasm and keenness to work with the new organization.

Considering a counter offer

If you decide to accept the job offer you need to let your current employer know your intention to leave. At that point there is a good chance you will receive a counter offer designed to persuade you to stay. It costs a lot of money to recruit someone new, and this may be a cost your line manager doesn't want to see blowing the staff budget so near to the financial year-end. Their performance review could be affected by staff turnover rates and so your resignation could be the final straw that turns their bonus from a hefty pay boost to a fairly paltry sum.

So what do you do if the employer comes back and offers a 5 per cent rise?

Negotiating chips

You can use the counter offer to strengthen your hand in negotiations with your new employer. In one case, a young accountant was offered a job with a salary of £32,000. He resigned and his current employer came back with a counter offer of £35,000. The new company offered £36,000, the existing employer fired back with £37,000 and finally the new company won the bidding with a £40,000 offer. This may not be the norm, but it shows how market forces can be put to good work in boosting an individual's pay.

What if you are tempted to stay?

Say the new employer doesn't up its pay package to beat your current employer's counter offer. You might be tempted to stay where you are and take the extra cash. However, any counter offer should always be assessed with a calm, analytical head.

Kickstart Tip

Experience shows that when people remain with their current employer after accepting a counter offer, the majority of them are on the job market again within the year.

Why is this? One key reason is that financial issues were usually only part of the reason the individual was looking for a new job in the first place. Desire for change, new challenges and extra promotion possibilities may have been key drivers behind the initial interest in finding a new job; being paid more but remaining in the same environment often proves only satisfactory in the short term.

Non-financial issues

The real value of the counter offer depends on how completely it meets all your current career needs. If the employer asks what it will take to persuade you to stay, explain clearly what you are looking for. If greater commercial exposure or staff management responsibility is on your list, ask for it. The employer may be so keen to keep you that a way will be found to give you these opportunities. Although you may have asked for these changes or this pay rise in the past, it may be only now that you are threatening to leave that the internal bureaucracy moves into action to meet your needs. If your line manager is screaming at personnel, 'We've got to keep this guy' or 'This woman is the lynchpin of my sales team', you could get a positive result.

If that happens, and the organization comes up with a solution that gives you a chance to develop your career in a desirable way, then the counter offer is seriously worth considering. As we said at the beginning of this book – the job-hunting process is an inherently risky process. Staying with an employer you know is generally less risky than moving to a new organization, which may have hidden faults. If you leave, you might be jumping from the frying pan into the fire. But what if you are given assurances that your role will be changed, but not yet? You may, for example, be told that room will be made for you in another department, but in six months' time when someone else moves on. Then you will have to make a judgement on how likely it is that the organization will be able to deliver its proposed solution. If your current employer is simply trying to stall your departure, perhaps to cope with an immediate staff shortage, and really has no intentions of meeting your wider career needs beyond a token pay rise, you would probably be wise to ignore the counter offer and move on to pastures new.

You should also bear in mind the potential damage caused by the rupture of trust; having once threatened to leave, your employer's belief in your loyalty will inevitably be weakened. Even if you decide to stay with the organization, your employer may well start viewing you as someone more likely to resign in future and may, as a result, not consider you first in line for the best projects or most challenging work.

Mr Gary Lane
Director of Finance and Administration
CableConnect

Dear Mr Lane

I am delighted to accept your offer of the position of Facilities Manager at CableConnect.

I believe I can make an important contribution to the success of the company and relish the challenge of creating a new department that meets the needs of a growing business.

I am contractually obliged to give my current employer three months notice but I am hopeful of negotiating a compromise period of just six weeks. In the meantime, subject to my current commitments, I would be happy to review the plans of the new Bristol office and to speak directly with the various office equipment suppliers. Can I suggest we meet early evening next week to discuss my initial job priorities? If your IT Manager is available we could also discuss the cabling requirements for the new Bristol location.

I am sure there will be minor details to sort out in relation to my starting work. Perhaps you would let me know whether I should speak to Human Resources or to you about these.

I look forward to receiving a full contract of employment for my position as soon as it is available.

Yours sincerely

Mark Carter

Mark Carter

Figure 16.1 A sample acceptance letter

Decision time

If you have any doubts about any issue associated with your potential new job, try to get an answer quickly. You can probably take a week to decide whether to accept a job offer, so don't waste time. If you need more time, perhaps because you are holding out for an offer from another, preferred organization, you should state a date when you will reply. The more professional your approach, the better the impression the organization will have of you if and when you do ultimately join its staff.

Once you decide that a particular job offer meets your requirements – in terms of your original job-hunting aims, overall career blueprint, cultural preferences and financial expectations – you can then draft your formal acceptance letter (see Figure 16.1 on p. 249 for an example). And open the champagne!

Chapter summary: key points

- You should assess your job offer thoroughly before you accept it.
- Consider how well it matches your original job-hunting aims and your overall career blueprint.
- Has your experience during the application process changed any initial judgements you made about the organization?
- How well does its culture fit you?
- Minimize the risk involved in moving to the new employer by seeking assurances on any key issues related to the new job.
- Clarify any contractual terms that worry you, particularly restrictive covenants, taking legal advice if necessary.
- Try to gain answers on any queries or doubts you have that are relevant to your decision.
- Don't be afraid to ask for more money if your request is rational and justified.
- Prepare for salary negotiations by valuing your current total pay and benefits package.
- You could expect a 10 to 25 per cent pay increase on changing employers.
- Find out what the market rates are for your sector and seniority level.
- Make use of any recruitment consultancy's skills, at least in initial negotiations.
- Be wary of counter offers that may only delay your eventual departure from your old employer.
- A salary increase alone may not be enough to justify staying in an unfulfilling role.
- Try to decide whether to accept the job offer within one week of receiving it.

Chapter 17

Saying Goodbye

So you've received your new job offer in writing and decided you want to go for it. It's an exciting time. However, you can't start your new job until you leave your old one, which means you need to hand in your notice and organize your affairs.

The art of resigning professionally

Maybe you've been overworked, underpaid and generally messed around in your old job. The thought that you can now leave this hellhole behind fills you with glee, and maybe even the desire for revenge on your boss. You imagine yourself marching up the corridor, storming into the poor manager's office, striking a dramatic pose and declaring with a flourish, 'I quit!' You can see the scene: your boss's mouth falls open, his face filled with horror and regret . . . Stop! This may be the stuff of a low-budget B-movie, but not of good career management.

It is important to resign with as much professionalism as you can. First, this is essential for your own networking interests. Second, you're probably going to have to work out a notice period, so why antagonize someone who could still make your working life difficult for the next month, maybe even longer?

Resigning with style can do much to add to your personal and professional credibility.

The importance of keeping good contacts

Your old boss can still have an impact on your career even after you've gone; you don't want him bad-mouthing you to your former colleagues or to his fellow managers. News of people leaving can make for good office gossip, particularly if that individual leaves in a storm. Word does travel and someone who doesn't really know you could get a bad impression of you. Whether that's unjustified or not doesn't really matter; the damage can easily be done, regardless of the facts.

Given that people move around between employers far more than they used to, it's quite possible that your path might cross with one of these people in future, or even with your old boss. Getting a reputation for leaving employers in the lurch will do you no good. You don't want to miss out on your dream job because someone once heard bad things about you.

Apart from trying to minimize any damage to your reputation and obtaining the reference you want, resigning with consideration for the employer you leave behind can positively enhance it. If people naturally associate you with concepts such as responsibility, consideration and professionalism, that can only be good news for you.

Remember the importance of networking. You may be sick of the sight of your old boss. You may feel that you have nothing in common personally, but you are still linked by your career histories and by the sectors in which you work. One day you may find yourself wanting information on a career move on which this person can advise, or where they could help open doors by using their other contacts. Be wise to the ways of the world, and the world will respond. Treat everyone fairly, and the chances are that others will be fair to you.

References

Another key reason why you should always try and create a good impression is that you will have a regular need for references as you move through your career. The boss you found difficult to work for may actually be a highly impressive referee.

To get the best from your referees, you should:

- select people who will give a good report of your abilities;
- ask them in advance;
- brief them on the job you are seeking and why you think you have received the job offer; and
- consider trying to use them at an early stage in your job search.

Most employers will want two references. Do not give more referees than are asked for. Even though they don't always go to the trouble of actually acting on these references, if they do, you want them to be good. The best way to make sure you always get a good reference is to always do a good job. Shoddy workers could be in trouble.

Choose your referees well

When deciding who to ask, pick wisely. Your referees should never be relatives, friends or peers. However, you don't have to name the head of your department. You simply have to name someone more senior than yourself. Obviously, you want to choose an individual who you are confident has a positive impression of your abilities, who you feel sure will give a favourable account of the work you have done.

The prospective new employer may expect one of these people to be the individual you currently report to; if you don't wish to use this person, you may need to be prepared to explain why not, perhaps because you have been working on a number of special projects recently, resulting in less contact than normal with your line manager. In any case, one of your referees should be employed in your current organization.

Briefing your referees

Clearly you need to approach your chosen individuals to ask them if they are happy to act as referees for you and to warn them that they may be contacted soon. It is probably also sensible to tell them what the job is you have applied for, and even to stress why you think the employer is interested in you. 'I told them about the marketing campaign I managed for you and how the response exceeded our projections. They are also very keen to establish the extent of my project management skills, so it would be great if you could mention that I managed to complete the preparatory stages ahead of time, despite being short-staffed in the department.'

Kickstart Tip

If you think you might help your chances by highlighting a particularly good recommendation, you can suggest to your recruitment consultant that they speak to your referees; this can help boost the consultant's belief in you as a marketable job seeker. Then the recruiter, or you yourself if you are not using a consultancy, can suggest that your interviewers also contact your referees, even before they consider offering you the job. A strong endorsement could be the vital factor that persuades them to offer you the desired position.

Maximizing referees' impact

If you think that a particular referee will be absolutely glowing about you, then you might want to use this person early in the recruitment process. For example, say your greatest asset is your technical ability on the job, but you don't come over particularly well in interview. One candidate had just this problem; he was rather scruffy and not particularly articulate when responding to interview questions. However, his former employer was happy to endorse him, describing him as the 'best systems accountant I have ever come across'. This backing was highly persuasive to potential recruiters.

The resignation letter

The first key to resigning professionally is to do it in writing. This indicates to the employer that your decision to resign is a serious one. If your boss subsequently persuades you to stay, you can always rip the letter up.

The resignation letter doesn't need to be long, but should cover the following areas:

- **The fact that you are leaving**
  Formally state that you are handing in your notice, while complying with the terms of your employment contract. If your contract contains a long notice period, you may want to ask whether there is any flexibility in that. However, stress that you will do all you can to support the department during the period up to your departure.

- **A reason for your departure**
  You don't need to go overboard on detail, nor do you have to give the most crucial reason. For example, try not to give an explanation that shows the organization you are leaving in a bad light; you may have finally decided to look for a new job because you just couldn't stand your new team leader, but it's better not to record that in writing. Instead you might just say you have accepted an offer for a position that will develop your career more quickly and which provides the new challenges you now seek.

- **A reference to the experience you have gained with this employer**
  This adds a positive note to the resignation letter. You could also thank your manager for their help along the way.

Once you have written the letter, put it in an envelope but don't leave it in an in-tray. You should hand it over in person, so request some time for a meeting with your boss. The request, 'Can I have a word?', will probably convey the fact that something is up. This meeting provides the forum for you to deliver the letter, which is essentially a summary of the discussion you will then have face to face.

Your boss will naturally be curious to hear more about the job you are going to and your reasons for leaving. Having prepared your letter should have helped shape your answers to the inevitable questions.

Wherever possible, be as open about your new employer and job role as possible, but keep your answers short without being curt. In most cases, your boss will wish you well. The immediate concern will be to minimize the inconvenience – personal and organizational – that your departure causes.

Be prepared for the fact that, unless your boss really doesn't like you or needs to make staff redundant anyway, the chances are they will want to see if you can be persuaded to stay. Recruiting a replacement is expensive, time-consuming and riskier than holding onto a known quantity – you.

Mr Paul Watt
Marketing Director
BLC

Dear Paul

I write to inform you of my decision to resign from my position as Marketing Manager. I have very much enjoyed my four years at BLC, but I believe I am now ready to step into a Marketing Director's role. The opportunity at Globe Metro also allows me to gain further international experience.

In accordance with my contract I am giving the requisite three months notice. However, if possible I would like to join my new employer on 14 June in order to attend a conference in the United States.

I have put together a schedule of my outstanding projects and my recommendations for handover. I believe that this can be successfully accomplished within the next seven weeks. If necessary, however, I would be more than happy to come in to BLC after work to deal with any outstanding items and, of course, I will always be available on the telephone to answer any queries.

I would like to express my sincere thanks for your continued help, guidance and support. I appreciate the faith you have always shown in me and for the learning opportunities you have given me.

I believe I have been able to make a significant contribution to the growth and development of BLC particularly in the areas of branding and e-marketing.

Lastly, if you require any assistance in recruiting my replacement I would be happy to assist. I have redrafted an up-to-date job description which includes my extended responsibilities.

With best wishes,
Yours sincerely

Terence Hoyte

Terence Hoyte

Figure 17.1 A sample resignation letter

However, remember the advice in Chapter 16, Negotiating the Best Job Offer, where we looked at assessing the counter offer. You may find yourself tempted to stay by the offer of more cash, but that probably won't satisfy your need for change for long.

The handover process

Whenever leaving a position within an organization, or the organization itself, it is important to make the transition from you to your successor as smooth as possible. Apart from helping the organization to operate efficiently, this approach ensures you leave a good impression behind.

To achieve a smooth handover, you should:

- consider how to handle any changeover issues before handing in your resignation;
- carry on working as normally as possible until you finally leave;
- volunteer to help find a successor, if relevant; and
- offer to be available to answer any queries after you have gone.

If you want to try and leave more quickly than your contractual notice period requires, you could also try to identify:

- potential barriers to your early departure and potential solutions;
- key projects that really require you to complete them; and
- colleagues who might be able and willing to take on some other aspects of your role.

How complex the handover is clearly depends on the job in question, whether the replacement is found before you leave and the extent to which the organization has procedures in place for handling such situations.

Early planning

It is wise to start thinking about changeover issues before your resignation meeting. You could prepare a schedule, separate from your resignation letter, that outlines any potential handover challenges, your current work in progress and any other issues you think relevant to planning a smooth departure.

Of course, some organizations may prefer you to go quickly, even immediately, if you are joining a direct competitor, although they may insist you spend time on gardening leave rather than letting you go to work for the rival straightaway. If you think there's a chance that you may be asked to leave the building immediately after you resign, make sure you've tidied your desk, packed or even already removed any personal items and sorted out any particularly pressing items before you hand over your resignation letter.

Business as usual

Assuming that you aren't frogmarched from the premises as soon as your resignation letter is read, you should try to carry on as normal a working routine as possible until you actually leave. It may be hard to keep your mind fully on the job, but you won't be popular with your colleagues if you start slacking and letting them carry you as you cruise towards your leaving do. Try to tie up loose ends and ensure all paperwork is in order and easily identifiable to your successor.

Help with succession issues

You could even volunteer to take part in finding a suitable successor. Maybe you think it's time to update the job spec that applied when you took the post. Such offers of help will not necessarily be taken up, but if they are, you should keep your word and be as helpful as possible.

Making yourself available

Whether or not you are leaving before your contract legally requires, you create a particularly good impression if you offer to be available to answer queries after you leave. If the handover is a particularly complex one, you could even volunteer to come back for a couple of evenings, but do not feel you have to. Obviously you don't really want to do this, but if it enables you to leave more quickly, it may be worth the compromise. If, however, the amount of work on the handover becomes too much, you should make your boss aware that it might not be possible to deal with all the issues. Your former employer may suggest you help out on a consultancy basis after you have left. Before agreeing to such an idea, check exactly what would be involved and ensure you obtain your new employer's agreement in advance, but be prepared for such a request to be refused.

Trying for a speedy exit

Many employees will be on a month's notice, although the more senior the position, the more likely that notice period will stretch to three or six months, or even a year. As mentioned above, it may be possible to negotiate a more rapid departure. You shouldn't try to pressurize your boss into agreeing to this, however. If you want to try and negotiate a speedy exit you need to give some thought to your bargaining chips.

Kickstart Tip

You could identify any key projects where your involvement is particularly vital. Can they be completed more quickly? Could you brief one of your colleagues to take on this particular responsibility? If you are contractually required to stay three months, but want to get out in six weeks, you could try drawing up a timetable that shows how you could complete essential projects in the shorter time frame.

The employer's main concern will be to avoid any problems, such as other staff being overloaded in a gap before your replacement is appointed, projects being delayed or clients being unavoidably let down. If you identify in advance all the areas where your departure could cause potential problems, and then come up with suggested solutions wherever possible, your case for early contractual release will be enhanced. If you are seen to be trying to help the employer, then the employer is more likely to try to help you.

If your employer won't agree to let you leave before the end of your notice period, you could decide to walk out anyway. No one can actually stop you from doing this. However, you must consider this option very carefully. There should be a good reason behind such an action because the company you are leaving probably won't take it kindly, not least because they will not want to set a precedent. Just because your new employer puts pressure on you to leave early, do not make a rash decision; you must review all the pros and cons. You do not want to gain a reputation for breaking contracts unnecessarily. Your current boss or company must be doing something that makes your life difficult, but whether it will be sufficient legitimately to entitle you to leave early will need careful consideration and legal advice.

The main risk, apart from potentially blowing away useful future references, is that you could find yourself on the wrong end of an action to compensate the employer for losses or costs incurred as a result of your early departure. Say, for example, you leave early and your employer brings in expensive temporary cover. If your old employer is seriously displeased with you, you could find yourself easily facing a claim for perhaps £15,000. If you think there is any risk this could happen, you must make sure your new employer pays for your legal advice and indemnifies you; you should not walk out early unless you have the complete and contractual support of your new employer, following a full and frank discussion with them and with a legal adviser instructed by you. (Do not rely on your new employer's legal adviser, who will be working for that company.)

Another risk from leaving early, particularly if you are heading for a rival organization, is that your old employer could try to take out an injunction to prevent you from starting your new job until the time when your notice period would have ended. If this happens, there is relatively little you can do except bide your time.

Speedy exits requested by the employer

If you are asked to leave early, or immediately, ask for a letter setting out exactly what you are being asked to do, both in terms of your contract and dealing with any ongoing work issues. In particular, you should ask for details of any pay you will receive in lieu of working out your notice period or part of it. Remember that if your employer requests your early departure you are still entitled to all the benefits you would have received had you stayed for the full period of your notice, not just to your salary.

If you are asked to leave early with pay in lieu of working out your notice period, it is particularly important that you try to find out what your former boss, if one of your referees, is going to say about you. Try to obtain a written reference before you leave or the promise to provide a reference, obtaining a broad and favourable outline of what it will contain.

Exit interviews

Some organizations like their HR departments to interview leavers. The aim is to hear first-hand why the individual is leaving, establish whether anything more could have been done to retain that person and gain some insight into the employee's general impression of life working in their department.

Handling such interviews can be tricky, depending on your reasons for leaving and your experiences in the organization. You don't want to lay into anyone, but what if there is a particular individual who has been damaging morale in your old department? What if you know that other staff members are planning to leave unless things improve? You might feel a sense of duty to tell the HR team about this problem in order to help your colleagues, who may themselves be unwilling to complain for fear of repercussions.

Such a decision has to be up to you. However, it is probably in your best interests to be fairly guarded about what you say. If the HR department acts on your information, the fact that you were the trigger may be obvious to any individual who is subsequently queried or challenged. Could this affect your references? Where possible, try to phrase any comments in diplomatic and fairly general terms. It is, after all, the HR department's job to identify HR problems, not yours.

The final departure

When you finally leave your old employer, don't get confused about what is your personal property and what is the employer's. Your notes on projects, your sales files – these belong to the organization; you should leave such hard copy versions of the intellectual capital you have generated behind. Don't try to take it with you.

Finally, celebrate if possible. Most people like to wave off a departing colleague, particularly over a few drinks in a local bar. It gives them, and you, an opportunity to formally acknowledge your time spent working together, and to exchange mutual thanks. And if you exchange such words over a good pint or glass of wine, that's even more guaranteed to leave your old colleagues with a good taste in the mouth.

After you've physically left the company, you might consider writing a couple of letters – to your old boss and your department. The letters shouldn't be smarmy, or disingenuous. You can simply thank your former colleagues for their help during the time you spent there, express the hope that you contributed to the organization and wish everyone well for the future. Repeat your offer of help if someone has a query related to taking on your work. Such consideration is unusual, but reinforces the impression that you are someone who goes the extra mile.

Chapter summary: key points

- Resigning professionally enhances your personal and professional reputation.
- Remember that the people you leave behind could be good contacts for your future career development.
- Pick your referees with care.
- Brief your referees on why you think you are suitable for your new job.
- Prepare a resignation letter that states you are leaving, gives a non-contentious explanation and refers briefly to the experience you have gained with this employer.
- Deliver the letter in person and be prepared to talk through your reasons for leaving in more detail.
- Do as much as you can to facilitate a smooth handover to your successor.
- Carry on working normally until you leave.
- If you want to exit more quickly, try to offer solutions to any barriers that could prevent you. For example, draw up a schedule of work that ensures any essential projects are completed.
- Make sure you take legal advice and are indemnified by your new employer if you decide to walk out early without your old employer's agreement.
- If you think you will be asked to leave the building immediately, have your desk in order before you resign.
- If you are asked to leave before the end of your notice period, obtain written clarification of the situation from your old employer, including your pay and benefits due.
- Be cautious about what you say at any exit interview.
- Don't try to take away your old employer's property when you finally leave.
- Consider writing to thank your former boss and colleagues for their support after you have left.

Chapter **18**

New Beginnings

From the moment you accept the offer of a job from a new employer, your emotional ties with your current workplace start to loosen. Although it is important to continue doing a decent job for your old organization, it is natural that your attention will start to drift towards the place that will be your new working home.

The interim period between finally leaving your old job and starting your new one is a time of emotional as well as real transition.

Deepening your knowledge

Throughout this book we have stressed that thorough research holds the key to success in the career game – when targeting likely employers, making speculative enquiries and preparing for interviews. Such research creates an understanding of the target organization, its market, its competitors and culture and puts you in a position of strength.

Having arrived at the end of the job-hunting process and accepted an offer of employment, you should already know a lot about the organization you are about to join. However, in the period before you actually cross the threshold as an employee for the first time, you should maintain your researcher's approach, looking out for any news reports in the press that refer directly to the organization or its sector. In this way you become increasingly attuned to your new environment and the issues that affect it.

In conducting your earlier research you may well have already studied the most recent company accounts, or flicked through the company's marketing brochures. If you haven't done so, this would be a good time to get hold of them and familiarize yourself with the company's recent progress. The annual report and accounts, for example, will give you brief biographies of the directors, so you will know what names to look out for.

You could also ask your new employer whether there is any other relevant information, not publicly available, that may be useful for your future role. There may, for example, be some form of office handbook or manual that you could start looking through to make sure you get up to speed fast once you finally start work in the organization.

Establishing relationships

During the interview process you will obviously have met a few people from the organization, and almost certainly your immediate boss. You might want to arrange another meeting – perhaps at lunchtime, or early evening over a drink – to get to know each other a bit better.

Kickstart Tip

If there are any departmental get-togethers involving your future colleagues, you could ask to come along so you can meet everyone in a less formal environment than in the office on day one of your appointment.

You could perhaps combine a couple of these options by popping into your new office at the end of an afternoon, to have another look round, see what projects people are working on, and then join them for a quick drink.

Suggesting such meetings will help to confirm in your new colleagues' minds that you are an enthusiastic individual who is looking forward to working with them. This helps to create a positive impression of you, even before you have officially started work there.

Such initial positive impressions can prove extremely helpful when you begin getting to grips with the working practices of the new organization. When you first start your job, people will give you perhaps a little more benefit of the doubt before making up their minds as to whether you are a valuable addition to the team. They may also be a little more willing to help you settle in if they have already met you and sensed your willingness to get to know them.

Remember how much there is to take in when you first start a new job: names and roles of those in your immediate team; names and roles of people your team interacts with; senior management personnel and directors; key clients; key suppliers; support staff; working practices, computer systems, and all the little office routines that create the organization. You will have a lot of new information thrown at you fast, and so the more familiar you can be with the office environment before you start, the better.

Start as you mean to go on

The quicker you can get off the mark in terms of understanding the office and your role in it, the better. At the end of your first three months, most people will have formed an impression of you that will be hard to change. You want them to start with a positive impression and for that impression to be reinforced as they get to know you.

That positive impression can be helped by simply making sure you get to work on time, dress appropriately to the office and display a positive, willing attitude from the start.

When you first join, it may be useful to make notes on the things that people tell you. Your colleagues will probably not mind repeating information once, but having to do so constantly will quickly annoy them. They have their own work to do and the quicker you are up to speed, the better for them.

That said, if there are elements of your new job that are unknown to you, or complex, ask about them as soon as you have questions. Your colleagues and your boss will understand that and expect you to have such questions in the early period after you join; but after a couple of months they may wonder why you didn't ask earlier, or worse, begin to doubt your ability to cope. Asking questions is after all a sign of an inquiring mind, and so can only confirm in people your commitment to doing the job well.

Probationary periods

How you handle yourself in the first few months is clearly vital if your employer requires you to work a probationary period before your job is actually confirmed. In Chapter 16, where we looked at how to assess the offer, you should have checked how the probationary period works. This means you should know how you will be judged, by whom, what determines your success or failure and what support will be made available to you to help you achieve the necessary performance level.

The fact that a probationary period exists can put some people off. You should try not to focus on it. Be aware that it is there, but beyond that, do the best job you can, as you would anyway.

> ### Kickstart Tip
>
> If you do have to complete a probationary period, make a point of seeking regular feedback from your boss – presumably the person who will have the final say on your performance – as to how you are doing and whether you are on track. If you are having particular difficulty in certain areas, focus on trying to get these up to speed. Be prepared to put in the extra effort required to get on top of what you are doing.

Remember that your boss and new colleagues will, unless they take a sudden dislike to you or find you a burden on the team, be rooting for you to succeed. Your boss certainly won't want to have to admit that he made a mistake recruiting you, nor have to go through the hassle of recruiting someone new all over again. People will be on your side, so make the most of their goodwill and ask for help and advice when you need it.

If at the end of the probationary period there are still some areas where you are a little shaky, if you have shown a keen attitude, willingness to learn and demonstrated a gradually improving performance, the chances are you will have earned enough plus points to be passed through and welcomed as a permanent member of the team.

Goal-setting

Starting your new job marks the fulfilment of your job-hunting goal. It also marks the point where you can draw up your new goals going forward.

When you finally join the new organization, keep gently in mind the key factors that drew you there. What new challenges were you hoping for? What new skills or attributes were you looking to develop? Your task now is to try and make these aims come true.

Any requests to develop your job role from the original outline should obviously be phrased politely, enthusiastically and with the willingness to help find solutions to any barriers impeding such change.

Alongside shaping your new role to be the one that fulfils your current needs, you can also start looking ahead to where you want the role to take you. As you settle into the organization you will develop a sense of how appropriate the culture there really is for you. If it fits like a glove, you may be happy to start aiming for further career progression within the organization, assuming there are attractive opportunities there. Even if the cultural match isn't quite perfect, you will want to spot ways that you can achieve some promotion or enhancement of your role. When the time comes to move on you will want to impress your next potential employer with the fact that your talents were recognized and developed.

Kickstart Tip

In your interview or at a post-offer meeting, your new line manager may have said there were indeed opportunities for you to take on some staff training responsibilities. This is important to you, but it was not something your predecessor did and the chances are that unless you raise the idea again with your manager, it will remain just that – an idea rather than a reality. Don't delay asking about such issues; make sure you raise them before your colleagues start assuming you are happy just to take on the role of your predecessor in the same way.

It makes sense to write down your immediate, medium and long-term goals before you start your new job. Three months in, you might want to look back and check whether you are getting what you initially desired from your role. If not, that's a good time to try and change things for the better for you.

Just ask

In initially shaping your role and later, in pushing for promotion, remember that those who don't ask, don't get. It's a point that runs true throughout this book. If you are job-hunting and you don't ask your friends and contacts for information, you severely limit your chances of success. If you want a slightly higher pay offer or slightly different benefits, you won't get them unless you ask.

Don't be afraid of a negative answer. Being rejected is better than feeling frustrated because your working life isn't delivering what you hoped.

So be bold. Aim high, and be prepared to work hard to achieve your dreams. There are so many exciting opportunities out there. Why not make sure it's you who is making the most of them?

Chapter summary: key points

- Make effective use of the time after you resign from your old job, before starting your new one.
- Follow any news stories about your new employer that appear in the press.
- Read up on company publications, such as marketing material and the report and accounts, if you haven't already done so.
- You might suggest meeting up with your future boss to get to know each other better.
- Consider arranging to visit your new office again, before you officially start there.
- Try to get up to speed as quickly as possible.
- Don't be afraid to ask questions about office routines and working practices.
- If you have to complete a probationary period, make sure you fully understand what is required of you and how your performance will be judged.
- Ask for regular feedback on how you are doing.
- If you want to adapt your new job specification in some way, raise the issue sooner rather than later.
- Set yourself some new career goals – for the short, medium and long-term future.

Appendix

Recruitment associations

Recruitment and Employment Confederation
36–38 Mortimer Street
London W1W 7RG
Tel: 020 7462 3260
Website: www.rec.uk.com

The following are specialist divisions of the REC:

Association of Online Recruiters
36–38 Mortimer Street
London W1W 7RG
Tel: 020 7462 3260
Website: www.aolr.org

Association of Search and Selection Consultants
36–38 Mortimer Street
London W1W 7RG
Tel: 020 7462 3260
Website: www.rec.uk.com/specialist/assc/assc.asp

Interim Management Association (formerly ATIES)
36–38 Mortimer Street
London W1W 7RG
Tel: 020 636 7166
Website: www.interimmanagement.uk.com

Pay and benefits specialists

Incomes Data Services
77 Bastwick Street
London EC1V 3TT
Tel: 020 7250 3434
Website: www.incomesdata.co.uk

The Reward Group
Reward House
Diamond Way
Stone Business Park
Stone
Staffordshire ST15 0SD
Website: www.reward-group.co.uk

Towers Perrin
Castlewood House
77–91 New Oxford Street
London WC1A 1PX
Tel: 020 7379 4411
Website: www.towers.com

Anti-discrimination and equal opportunities bodies

Campaign Against Age Discrimination in
Employment
395 Barlow Road
Altrincham
Cheshire WA14 5HW
Tel: 0161 941 2902
Website: www.caade.net

Commission for Racial Equality
Elliot House
10–12 Allington Street
London SW1E 5EH
Tel: 020 7828 7022
Website: www.cre.gov.uk

Disability Rights Commission
DRC Helpline
Freepost MID 02164
Stratford-upon-Avon
Warwickshire CV37 9BR
Tel: 08457 622 633
Website: www.drc-gb.org

Equal Opportunities Commission
Customer Contact Point
Arndale House
Arndale Centre
Manchester M4 3AQ
Tel: 0161 833 9244
Website: www.eoc.org.uk

Useful references

Helen Barrett (editor), *Executive Grapevine:
The Grapevine Index of Senior Human Resource
Professionals: 2000/2001*, Executive Grapevine
(2000).

Corporate Research Foundation, *Britain's Top
Employers: A Guide to the Best Companies to Work
For*, HarperCollins Business (1999).

Mary Spillane *Branding Yourself*, Pan (2000).

Index